King Baldwin IV

Dedication

To the memory of King Baldwin IV, the Lion of Jerusalem, a testament to courage, resilience, and leadership in the face of extraordinary adversity. His life, though tragically short, serves as a powerful reminder that even amidst debilitating illness and relentless political intrigue, the human spirit can triumph. This book is dedicated to his enduring legacy and to all those who, like him, have overcome seemingly insurmountable obstacles to achieve greatness. It is also dedicated to the scholars and researchers whose tireless efforts have illuminated the past, allowing us to understand and appreciate the complexities of the medieval world and the remarkable individuals who shaped its history. Their work, a testament to the power of human inquiry, forms the foundation upon which this biography rests. Finally, this work is dedicated to my family and friends, whose love and support made the completion of this project possible. Their encouragement and understanding were invaluable throughout the long process of research, writing, and revision. This book would not have been possible without their unwavering belief in my ability to bring King Baldwin's story to life.

Preface

This biography of King Baldwin IV of Jerusalem aims to provide a comprehensive and engaging account of his life, reign, and lasting legacy. While numerous works have touched upon his story, this book seeks to offer a fresh perspective by weaving together a detailed narrative with rigorous historical analysis. It draws extensively on primary sources, including contemporary chronicles, letters, and other historical records, offering insights into the political, social, and military contexts of his time. Particular attention is given to the interplay between Baldwin IV's personal struggles with leprosy and his remarkable achievements as a military leader and political strategist. The narrative explores his complex relationships with family members, advisors, and rivals, highlighting the challenges he faced in maintaining control amidst internal and external conflicts. The book also analyzes the impact of his illness on both his personal life and the trajectory of the Kingdom of Jerusalem, examining how he adapted to his physical limitations and how his illness shaped his decision-making. The goal is not only to recount the events of his life but also to provide a nuanced and empathetic portrayal of a truly extraordinary individual whose story continues to captivate and inspire. The reader will find that, even after centuries, Baldwin's life offers valuable lessons in leadership, resilience, and the enduring power of the human spirit in the face of adversity. We will explore the nuances of the challenges he faced, and how he was ultimately shaped by his environment and legacy.

Introduction

King Baldwin IV of Jerusalem (1161-1185), a figure whose life was marked by both triumph and tragedy, stands as a compelling subject of historical inquiry. His reign, though relatively short, was a crucial period in the history of the Crusader states, a time of both significant military victories and profound internal conflicts. Born into the royal family of Jerusalem, Baldwin faced the devastating diagnosis of leprosy at a young age. This illness, viewed with fear and stigmatization in the medieval world, was not only a personal challenge but also presented significant political obstacles. Despite his physical limitations, he rose to become one of the most formidable military commanders of his era, achieving remarkable victories against the forces of Saladin. His strategic brilliance, coupled with his courage and determination, allowed him to defend the Kingdom of Jerusalem against overwhelming odds. However, Baldwin's story is not solely one of military success. His reign was also characterized by intricate courtly intrigues, power struggles, and the ever-present threat of internal dissent. His relationships with family members, particularly his sister Sibylla and her husband Guy de Lusignan, were fraught with tension, posing major obstacles to peaceful and secure succession. This biography will delve into these complexities, exploring the political landscape of twelfth-century Jerusalem and the multifaceted challenges that Baldwin faced. Through a careful examination of primary and secondary sources, the book aims to provide a multifaceted portrait of Baldwin IV—as a king, as a military leader, as a man grappling with a debilitating disease, and as a pivotal figure in a pivotal moment in history. By placing his life within its historical context, we will explore his enduring legacy, and how his accomplishments and struggles shaped both his time and history.

Chapter 1

The Early Years in Jerusalem Family Court and the First Signs of Illness

~~Chapter 1~~

Baldwin IV was born in Jerusalem in 1161, into the heart of a kingdom perpetually teetering on the brink of chaos. His arrival, while undoubtedly joyous for his parents, Amalric I, King of Jerusalem, and Agnes of Courtenay, was immediately entangled in the complex web of Crusader politics. The Kingdom of Jerusalem, a patchwork of fiefdoms carved from the Levant, was far from unified. Powerful noble families, often vying for influence and land, created a volatile atmosphere even before considering the ever-present threat of Muslim expansion. Amalric, a shrewd and capable king, constantly navigated these treacherous currents, ensuring the stability of his realm. His son's birth, therefore, carried not only the promise of future kingship but also the weight of considerable political expectations.

Baldwin's early years were spent within the opulent yet precarious environment of the royal court. The palace, a center of power and intrigue, buzzed with the constant activity of knights, prelates, administrators, and visiting dignitaries. Life at court, as described in various chronicles, was a vibrant tapestry of feasts, tournaments, and religious observances, punctuated by the ever-present undercurrent of political maneuvering. Young Baldwin, heir apparent to the throne, would have been exposed to this world from a young age, learning the art of diplomacy and statecraft through observation and participation. While undoubtedly educated in the classical subjects expected of a prince – Latin, literature, and perhaps even some aspects of philosophy – the emphasis of his training focused on the practicalities of kingship within the Crusader states. This meant a rigorous education in military strategy and tactics, coupled with extensive training in horsemanship and weaponry.

The exact nature of Baldwin's childhood is somewhat elusive, with a few primary sources offering intimate details of his daily life. However, fragments of information are scattered across chronicles and letters paint a picture of a royal upbringing that was both privileged and challenging. He would have had access to the finest tutors and enjoyed the comforts and luxuries available to the royal family. Yet, this idyllic existence was starkly contrasted by the inherent dangers of the time and the looming shadow of war with the powerful Muslim states that surrounded the Kingdom of Jerusalem.

The first signs of Baldwin's leprosy are shrouded in some ambiguity. While precise dates remain unclear in many sources, it is generally accepted that the disease manifested itself during his early childhood, perhaps around the age of five or six. The contemporary understanding of leprosy, now known as Hansen's disease, was far removed from our modern medical knowledge. It was considered a highly contagious and incurable affliction, often associated with divine punishment or spiritual impurity. Leprosy, therefore, carried a profound social stigma, isolating those afflicted and relegating them to the margins of society. The appearance of this debilitating disease in the young heir to the throne would have sent shockwaves through the court.

The medical treatments available in the 12th century were rudimentary at best and often ineffective. While some herbal remedies and religious practices might have been employed to treat the symptoms of leprosy, there was no known cure. The disease gradually progressed, causing disfigurement and physical impairment. For Baldwin, the onset of leprosy would have been not merely a medical crisis, but a profound personal and political challenge, altering the course of his life in ways that were unimaginable at the time. The immediate consequences were numerous and significant. Questions about the succession began to surface, as the prospect of a king incapacitated by disease threatened the very stability of the kingdom. The political landscape shifted, with various factions in the court jockeying for position and influence amidst the uncertainty. Court physicians, theologians, and advisors would have been engaged in heated debates concerning the implications of the king's son suffering from this dreadful disease.The impact of Baldwin's illness extended beyond the political sphere. His family, undoubtedly devastated by the news, would have experienced a profound emotional toll. The court itself responded with a mixture of fear, pity, and speculation. Many courtiers would have worried about the potential for contagion and perhaps about their own positions given the uncertainty about the future of the kingdom. Some may have seen this event as a sign of divine displeasure or a curse upon the royal house. The social implications of leprosy extended to daily life. While Baldwin remained part of the royal family, his interactions with others likely became more controlled to mitigate the risk of spreading the disease. The disease would have also had a significant impact on his education and training, potentially altering the nature and intensity of his preparation for kingship. Though he clearly received a thorough military and political education, as evidenced by his later skills, one can only imagine how the disease impacted his progress.

Beyond the immediate family and court, the news of the young prince's leprosy spread throughout the kingdom and likely beyond its borders. The disease, considered divinely ordained punishment in the medieval world, may have created fear among the populace. Some individuals may have reacted with fear and stigma, further highlighting the harsh reality of life with leprosy in the Middle Ages. Others, seeing the prince's fate, might have strengthened their religious faith, offering prayers for his health or viewing his affliction through a different spiritual lens. Regardless, the impact of this disclosure extended far beyond the walls of the palace, shaping perceptions of the royal family and influencing political dynamics within the Kingdom. This early affliction became a constant shadow, shaping Baldwin's life from childhood, testing his will, and ultimately influencing the course of his remarkable, albeit tragically short, reign. His story is not just about overcoming a debilitating disease, it is about his resilience in the face of political intrigue, external threats, and the ever-present weight of his royal responsibilities. It is this blend of personal and political drama that makes Baldwin IV a truly fascinating figure in medieval history.

Chapter 2

The Royal Lineage and Political Intrigue Surrounding his Birth

The birth of Baldwin IV in 1161 occurred against a backdrop of simmering tensions and intricate power struggles within the Kingdom of Jerusalem. Amalric I, his father, ruled a realm far from monolithic. The kingdom, a precarious patchwork of fiefdoms established through conquest, was a volatile mix of Frankish nobles, indigenous populations, and assorted religious orders, each with their own agendas and ambitions. The delicate balance of power rested precariously on Amalric's shrewd political maneuvering, a testament to his skills as a ruler, yet a constant reminder of the inherent instability of his kingdom.

Amalric's own lineage played a crucial role in shaping the political landscape. He was the son of Fulk of Anjou and Melisende, Queen of Jerusalem. His claim to the throne wasn't without its challenges, inheriting a kingdom where strong familial ties often intertwined with political ambitions. The death of his brother, Baldwin III, had smoothed his own ascension, but it highlighted the ever-present potential for succession crises, a pattern that would haunt his own reign and tragically echo in the life of his son, Baldwin IV.

The major noble houses of the Kingdom—the Ibelins, the Briennes, the Montferrats, and others—held considerable power and influence, often surpassing that of lesser lords. These families, through strategic marriages and shrewd alliances, had amassed vast territories and wealth, giving them significant leverage in courtly affairs. Their loyalty to the crown was often conditional, fluctuating based on perceived advantages and the shifting political winds. Their influence extended to nearly all aspects of governance, from military command to the administration of justice. Amalric, recognizing this delicate reality, had to navigate a complex web of familial connections and rivalries to maintain a semblance of stability.

The years preceding Baldwin's birth were marked by a series of internal power struggles, largely focused on the balance of power between the established families and the crown. The acquisition and distribution of lands, the allocation of key administrative and military positions, all became sources of contention, fueling tensions and creating alliances that shifted as circumstances demanded. Amalric, a skilled diplomat and military strategist, frequently played competing factions against one another, preventing any single house from becoming overwhelmingly powerful, while keeping enough of their support to secure his position. This constant political chess game, however, always held the potential to destabilize his kingdom, a situation complicated further by the constant external threats from the surrounding Muslim states.

The succession to the throne was always a sensitive issue, surrounded by speculation and intense competition. Amalric's marriage to Agnes of Courtenay, his second wife, was itself a calculated move designed to strengthen his position and secure his legacy. However, the birth of Baldwin IV was still met with a mix of relief and apprehension. Relief that the royal line would continue, but apprehension due to the complex succession procedures of the Kingdom. The traditional Salic law, which barred female inheritance, was not strictly observed in Jerusalem. The precedent of Melisende's reign had established that capable women could rule.

This meant that any daughters born to Amalric, or even potential claims from female relatives, could potentially disrupt the straightforward succession to Baldwin.

The death of Baldwin III, Amalric's brother, had been a relatively smooth transition of power, but it had not eliminated the potential for future instability. The noble families, ever watchful for opportunities to advance their own interests, would certainly assess the situation carefully following Amalric's death. A weak or incapacitated ruler presented an opportunity for those with ambition to exploit, leading to internal conflict or even foreign intervention. Therefore, the birth of Baldwin IV was not simply a family matter; it was a matter of immense political significance.

The very act of Baldwin's birth did little to resolve the underlying political tensions. In fact, the precarious health of the young prince immediately introduced a new layer of uncertainty. The onset of leprosy, though its precise timing remains debated by historians, became a pivotal moment in the ongoing power struggle within the

kingdom. The disease's emergence added fuel to the fire of political intrigue. The uncertainty surrounding Baldwin's ability to rule created a vacuum that ambitious nobles quickly attempted to exploit. The early years of his life, rather than representing a period of peace and stability, were marked by the constant, subtle jostling of political forces at court, each vying for influence over the young heir.

While Amalric, a seasoned politician, strove to maintain his control and project an image of stability, whispers of doubt and intrigue certainly circulated within the royal court. The disease immediately raised questions regarding the legitimacy of the succession. The traditional order of succession, already complex, has now become increasingly ambiguous. The seriousness of Baldwin's affliction cast doubt on his capacity to effectively govern, providing an opening for those seeking to advance their own claims. While Amalric publicly remained confident in his son's future, the shadow of uncertainty hung heavily over the court.

Amalric's own actions after Baldwin's illness became a critical element in shaping the political dynamics. His efforts to secure Baldwin's position as heir apparent, alongside his attempts to maintain stability amid the growing uncertainties, were all key strategies in managing this period of crisis. He likely employed a blend of concessions, strategic alliances, and perhaps some suppression of dissent to maintain a semblance of order. However, his efforts, while successful in the short term, ultimately only delayed the eruption of overt conflict that would ultimately shape the reign of Baldwin IV. The political machinations surrounding the young king's illness would not simply vanish; they would morph and adapt, evolving into the overt struggles and conspiracies that would define Baldwin IV's reign. The early years of his life were thus a microcosm of the challenges that faced the Kingdom of Jerusalem: a delicate balance of power constantly threatened by external and internal conflicts, a balance that his early illness dramatically destabilized, creating a stage for the profound political drama of his life.

Amalric's death in 1174 further exacerbated these existing tensions. Baldwin IV, still a child and already showing signs of the progression of his disease, ascended to the throne, and the fragile peace constructed by his father quickly unraveled. The various noble families, who had patiently waited for the right opportunity to advance their positions, now saw their chance. The young king's illness rendered him vulnerable, perceived as a relatively weak ruler, opening the door for power grabs and maneuvering by the ambitious lords of the realm. The next decade would be marked by repeated attempts to undermine Baldwin's authority, culminating in a protracted struggle for control of the kingdom, a struggle that would severely test the young king's resilience and ability to govern. The fragile peace that Amalric had managed to construct crumbled under the weight of ambition and the uncertainty surrounding the king's health, transforming Baldwin IV's reign into an intense and dramatic period in the history of the Crusader States.

The political scene, already fraught with complex alliances and rivalries, became even more unpredictable and volatile, setting the stage for a fascinating study of power, disease, and the enduring legacy of a king who ruled despite extraordinary odds.

Chapter 3

The Diagnosis and its Impact Social Stigma and Political Maneuvering

---------------------------Chapter 3------------------

~~T~~The diagnosis of leprosy, a disease shrouded in fear and misunderstanding in the medieval world, cast a long shadow over Baldwin IV's life and profoundly impacted the political landscape of the Kingdom of Jerusalem. While the precise moment of diagnosis remains uncertain, the knowledge of his affliction irrevocably altered the trajectory of his reign and the expectations surrounding his kingship. Leprosy, or Hansen's disease as it's known today, was not merely a medical condition; it was a social and political catastrophe. The disease's visible symptoms – skin lesions, nerve damage leading to deformities, and eventual disfigurement – led to widespread social ostracization. Medieval society, deeply rooted in religious beliefs, often viewed leprosy as a divine punishment for sin, a manifestation of God's wrath. This belief fostered a climate of fear and revulsion, contributing to the systematic marginalization of those afflicted.

Individuals diagnosed with leprosy were often forced into isolation, confined to leper colonies or lazar houses, effectively severed from their communities and families. This separation was not merely physical; it was deeply symbolic, representing a profound social death. Their status was marked by legal limitations, restrictions on property ownership, and the loss of various civil rights. Such individuals were treated as essentially non-persons, living on the fringes of society, their lives reduced to a state of liminality.
Baldwin IV, a young prince destined for the throne, found himself facing this dreadful reality. The diagnosis of leprosy immediately

raised profound questions about his fitness to rule, his very legitimacy as heir to the throne.

The implications for succession planning were immediate and significant. While the Kingdom of Jerusalem did not strictly adhere to Salic law, which excluded women from inheritance, the precedent of Melisende's reign had demonstrated that female claimants could, under certain circumstances, seize the throne. The emergence of Baldwin's illness, therefore, introduced a considerable element of uncertainty. Ambitious nobles, always watching for opportunities to advance their interests, saw in their condition a potential vulnerability, a fissure in the otherwise seamless line of succession. The question of who would succeed Baldwin, if he proved unable to rule, became a central point of intrigue and contention within the royal court.

The social stigma surrounding leprosy also drastically impacted Baldwin's court relationships. While his father, Amalric I, likely made every effort to maintain a semblance of normalcy, whispers and rumors undoubtedly circulated within the court, undermining the king's authority and fostering an environment of suspicion. The courtiers' behavior likely shifted subtly, a mixture of pity, fear, and opportunism shaping their interactions with the young prince.

Those who had previously been loyal courtiers might have calculated their actions differently given Baldwin's deteriorating health, seeing the need to reposition themselves for a future without him. Those who held a claim to the throne or believed they possessed the ability to ascend had a powerful incentive to cultivate allies, waiting for the moment where they could take advantage of the king's predicament.

The disease also had implications for the broader social structure of the kingdom. The uncertainty surrounding Baldwin's ability to rule created a vacuum of power, tempting several of the powerful aristocratic families to push their own agendas. The absence of a strong, healthy king created a power struggle not only over succession, but over the control of the kingdom's resources and the ability to influence the political decisions of the regency.

The impact extended beyond the immediate court. The news of the king's leprosy likely spread throughout the kingdom, potentially influencing the morale of the population and the loyalty of the vassal lords. The populace, deeply religious, might have viewed the disease as a divine judgment, questioning the legitimacy of the kingdom itself. This could have increased the vulnerability of the kingdom to external threats, like the ever-present Muslim states to the south and east. It might have also encouraged unrest among the population, fueled by fear and uncertainty. Baldwin's illness,
therefore, added a layer of complexity to the already precarious situation of the Crusader Kingdom.

Amalric's death in 1174 only intensified this precarious situation. The transition to Baldwin IV's reign was far from seamless. While the young king showed signs of strength and brilliance, his condition ensured his reign was a constant balancing act, a fight for control against the looming threat of his disease, and against the ambitious nobles vying for power. The early years of his reign would show the profound effect of both his illness and his character. His leprosy created a crisis of legitimacy, while his own determined spirit and political skill would, at least for a time, manage to maintain the kingdom's precarious balance.

The initial diagnosis, therefore, far from being a mere medical event, was a pivotal moment that reshaped the political and social fabric of the Kingdom of Jerusalem. It heightened existing tensions within the kingdom, creating further instability and uncertainty in the line of succession, and providing powerful incentives for ambitious nobles to engage in political intrigue and conspiracy. The stigma associated with leprosy further complicated this situation, impacting Baldwin's relationships and influencing his ability to rule effectively. The shadow of leprosy cast a pall over the kingdom's political life, shaping its trajectory in profound and unforeseen ways and impacting the lives of those closest to him in unimaginable ways.

The social ramifications extended beyond the personal sphere. The fear of contagion, fueled by religious interpretations of the disease, led to social isolation, limiting Baldwin's physical interactions with his court and his people. This isolation was both literal and metaphorical. The physical separation from his court, necessitated by the risk of infection, further hampered his ability to exert his authority and build lasting relationships of trust. This isolation, coupled with the fear and suspicion generated by his illness, also created an atmosphere conducive to rumors and conspiracies. The nobles, already eyeing opportunities to advance their positions, saw in this isolation an opening, a chance to undermine the king's authority and influence court decisions without his direct involvement.

This atmosphere of distrust was further exacerbated by the

changing political landscape of the Levant. The kingdom's external enemies were constantly observing the internal dynamics, eagerly waiting for an opportunity to exploit any perceived weakness. The perceived vulnerability brought on by Baldwin's condition offered a potentially irresistible opportunity for their ambitious neighbors.

Therefore, the diagnosis of leprosy wasn't merely a matter of personal affliction; it was a significant factor in the broader geopolitical landscape, impacting the kingdom's vulnerability to external threats and affecting its ability to maintain its precarious position within the region.

The reaction of the various noble families was multifaceted and often contradictory. Some expressed sympathy and offered support, potentially motivated by genuine concern or the expectation of future rewards. However, other noble houses were more opportunistic, sensing an opportunity to gain influence and power. They likely maneuvered subtly, exploiting the uncertainty caused by the king's illness and forming alliances to protect their interests and prepare for a potential succession crisis.

The young king, though burdened by the weight of his illness, demonstrated remarkable resilience and determination. He skillfully navigated the complexities of court politics and displayed astute military leadership, achieving significant military success despite his physical limitations. However, the ever-present shadow of his illness relentlessly threatened to undermine his efforts. The constant fear of his demise, the physical limitations of his condition, and the underlying political machinations made his reign an extraordinary exercise in statecraft and resilience.

In conclusion, the diagnosis of leprosy was a pivotal moment in the life of Baldwin IV, transforming his life and shaping the political fate of the Kingdom of Jerusalem. It was a diagnosis that not only impacted on his personal life but triggered a chain of events that reshaped the political, social, and even religious fabric of the Crusader kingdom, revealing the complex interactions between disease, social stigma, and power dynamics within medieval society. The young king's struggle against his illness and the political machinations of his court became a defining chapter in the history of the Crusader States, leaving a legacy of both tragedy and resilience.

Chapter 4

Military Training Amidst Adversity Forging a Kings Skills

Even before the full weight of his leprosy became apparent, Baldwin IV's upbringing was far from the idyllic existence one might associate with a royal prince. While he undoubtedly received the finest education available in the Kingdom of Jerusalem, encompassing literature, theology, and governance, a significant portion of his training focused on the martial arts. This was not merely a matter of tradition; it was a necessity. The Kingdom of Jerusalem was a perpetually precarious entity, clinging to existence amidst a sea of hostile Muslim powers. The king, regardless of age or physical condition, was expected to be a warrior-king, capable of leading his armies into battle and defending the realm.

For Baldwin, this imperative was amplified tenfold by the shadow of his impending illness. He understood, perhaps even earlier than his advisors, that his physical capabilities might soon be drastically compromised. This understanding fueled his relentless dedication to mastering horsemanship and swordsmanship. He trained not just to meet the expectations of his station, but to compensate for the inevitable physical limitations that his disease would impose.

His training regime was rigorous, demanding, and undoubtedly painful at times. The sources don't detail the specifics of his daily routine, but we can infer from the accounts of his later military successes that it must have been exceptionally demanding. He must have endured countless hours in the saddle, honing his skills in equestrian combat, learning to wield a lance with deadly precision while maintaining his balance and control. This was no mere pastime; it was grueling physical exertion, pushing his body to its limits, even as those limits were beginning to shrink.

His swordsmanship training was equally intense. He practiced with a variety of weapons, including the sword, mace, and possibly even the axe, learning the intricate techniques of medieval combat. The goal was not merely to wield a weapon effectively, but to master the art of

warfare, understanding strategy, tactics, and the psychology of battle. This involved not only physical prowess but also strategic thinking, the ability to anticipate the opponent's moves, and to adapt to the ever-changing circumstances of a battlefield.

The physical demands of this training were magnified by his progressive illness. The early stages of leprosy would have caused pain, numbness, and progressive loss of motor function, yet Baldwin persevered. He pushed himself beyond what most, even healthy individuals, could endure, exhibiting a remarkable level of determination and self-discipline. This is not merely admirable; it's crucial to understanding his later military successes. His mastery of warfare wasn't solely a matter of inherent talent; it was forged in the crucible of adversity, shaped by the relentless pressure of his physical deterioration.

His trainers, likely experienced knights and military instructors familiar with the harsh realities of warfare in the Levant, must have been impressed by his dedication and resilience. They would have adapted their methods to accommodate his physical limitations, while simultaneously pushing him to achieve a level of mastery that few could attain. This adaptation demonstrates a remarkable level of understanding and sensitivity. It was not simply a matter of teaching him to fight; it was about nurturing his strategic mind and adapting his training to his evolving physical capabilities.

Beyond the purely physical aspects of his training, Baldwin developed a sharp military intellect. He studied military history, analyzing past battles and campaigns, learning from the successes and failures of other commanders. He immersed himself in the strategic intricacies of warfare, understanding the importance of terrain, logistics, and troop deployment. This intellectual engagement was crucial, as it allowed him to compensate for any physical limitations he encountered on the battlefield. The intellectual preparation allowed him to lead his armies effectively, even as his physical condition declined.

His understanding of siege warfare, particularly noteworthy given the frequent sieges in the Crusader States, demonstrates the depth of his military education. He understood the importance of careful planning, siege weaponry, and troop movements in securing victories. The sources depict him as adept at planning sieges, using deception, and maximizing his limited resources. His strategies were often ingenious and effective, reflecting the keen strategic mind that he honed through years of study and relentless practice.

The impact of his leprosy on his training remains a subject of speculation, but its presence undoubtedly influenced the trajectory of his development as a warrior king. It's conceivable that certain aspects of his training were modified to accommodate his condition, potentially focusing on strategic thinking and leadership rather than purely physical combat skills. However, the evidence suggests that he actively compensated for his physical limitations, training relentlessly to achieve a high level of proficiency, refusing to allow his disease to define his capabilities.

The sources illuminate his strategic genius, his tactical acumen, and his almost preternatural ability to inspire loyalty and courage in his troops. This was not merely a consequence of his royal status. His deep understanding of warfare, coupled with his unwavering determination, earned him the respect of his men, who were willing to follow him into battle, even in the face of overwhelming odds, because of his proven skill and leadership.

This dedication to military training was not merely a preparation for his future role as king; it was a deeply personal response to the challenges posed by his disease. It was an act of defiance, a refusal to allow his leprosy to define him, to limit his potential, or to diminish his value as a ruler and a warrior. His training was a testament to his indomitable spirit, a symbol of his determination to overcome adversity and to lead his kingdom with skill and courage, despite the relentless shadow of his illness.

The rigorous training that Baldwin IV underwent was not simply a royal duty; it was a personal crusade, reflecting his relentless pursuit of mastery in the face of a debilitating illness. It was an act of self-affirmation, a declaration that he would not be defined by his affliction but would transcend it through unwavering determination and exceptional leadership. His early training, therefore, wasn't simply the foundation for his military prowess; it was the foundation for his entire reign, a testament to his unwavering resilience in the face of adversity. It is this strength of character, honed through years of rigorous physical and mental training amidst the constant shadow of leprosy, that would define his reign as King of Jerusalem. The training was not just physical; it was a forging of the character and mental fortitude that would enable him to navigate the turbulent political landscape and military challenges of his time. The adversity he faced during his training became the crucible from which his exceptional leadership emerged. The outcome of this training, developed in the face of his progressive illness, would prove crucial in the years to come, allowing him to lead his armies to victory against all odds.

Chapter 5

Early Challenges to the Regency Consolidating Power and Facing Opposition

The death of Amalric I in 1174 left the Kingdom of Jerusalem in a precarious position. His young son, Baldwin IV, was only thirteen years old, too young to effectively rule a kingdom beset by internal factions and external threats. A regency was established, a necessary but inherently unstable arrangement. The power vacuum created by Amalric's death immediately attracted ambitious individuals vying for influence and control. Raynald of Châtillon, Lord of Oultrejordain, a notoriously volatile and ambitious nobleman, posed a significant threat. His past actions, marked by reckless disregard for the kingdom's stability and alliances, already raised concerns among many barons. Raynald's independent actions, often taken without regard to the kingdom's best interests, were a source of consistent worry. His ambition seemed to outweigh any sense of loyalty to the crown, creating a volatile element within the regency.

The regency council, tasked with governing on Baldwin's behalf, was itself a battleground of competing interests. While ostensibly united in their duty to the young king, the various noble families represented held divergent agendas and ambitions. The council consisted primarily of powerful barons, each striving to further their family's influence. Their internal disputes frequently hampered effective governance, providing opportunities for external enemies to exploit the kingdom's internal divisions. The council's very composition, a reflection of the kingdom's complex power dynamics, inherently lacked unity and fostered a spirit of competition rather than cooperation.

The power struggles within the regency extended beyond simple disagreements over policy. The distribution of patronage, access to royal resources, and the allocation of military commands were all sources of intense conflict. Each decision taken by the regency was closely scrutinized by other members and rival factions, often leading to protracted negotiations and delays. This stagnation served to undermine the kingdom's effectiveness in both internal administration and external defense. A swift, decisive response to external threats were hampered by the slow decision-making processes inherent in such a fractured council.

Adding to the already unstable situation was the looming threat of Saladin, the powerful Kurdish leader who was consolidating his control over Egypt and Syria. Saladin represented a formidable enemy; far more capable and ambitious than any previous Muslim leader the Kingdom had faced. His military prowess, along with his shrewd political maneuvering, posed a significant threat to the Kingdom's very existence. The regency's internal squabbles hindered their ability to prepare for a potential conflict with Saladin, a critical failure in governance that could have devastating consequences. The fragmented nature of the regency council left the kingdom ill-equipped to face this powerful adversary.

The early years of Baldwin IV's reign were thus marked by a constant struggle to maintain control. The young king, even while still a minor, demonstrated a remarkable understanding of the political intricacies of his kingdom. He began to gradually assert his authority, albeit subtly at first. The delicate balance of power within the regency demanded careful maneuvering, and any misstep could trigger devastating conflict. Baldwin showed an early grasp of the power dynamics at play, skillfully navigating the treacherous terrain of courtly politics. He played factions against one another, skillfully exploiting their internal divisions to consolidate his position.

The young king's intelligence and political acumen were evident in his choice of advisors. He carefully selected individuals who could both advise him wisely and counterbalance the competing interests of the more powerful nobles. This strategic selection of loyal and capable advisors served to create a counterweight to the influence of other powerful magnates, limiting their capacity to exploit the political vulnerabilities caused by the regency. This careful selection was a demonstration of political maturity beyond his years.

This early phase was far from a calm period of consolidation. The internal conflicts, often fueled by personal ambitions and grievances, created numerous challenges for the young king. Several attempts to undermine the regency were documented, highlighting the fragility of the political situation. These included not only open rebellions, but also clandestine conspiracies designed to destabilize the kingdom. These attempts, though often suppressed, reveal the constant pressure Baldwin faced in maintaining his authority.

The regency was marked by several near misses, where even minor incidents could have led to open warfare amongst the kingdom's nobility. The fragility of the situation is evidenced by the numerous occasions on which disputes nearly escalated into armed conflict.

The various factions constantly tested the boundaries of their authority, leading to a heightened state of tension and a constant threat of open revolt. The regency system, while necessary, proved to be a volatile and unstable mechanism of governance, only barely managing to hold the kingdom together.

Despite the tumultuous political climate, Baldwin displayed a remarkable resilience and political skill. He successfully navigated the treacherous currents of courtly intrigue, slowly but surely consolidating his power base. The young king demonstrated not only an innate political acumen but also a remarkable ability to learn from his mistakes and adapt to the ever-shifting political landscape. His experiences within the context of the regency would serve as an invaluable education, equipping him with the skills and experience to navigate the complexities of royal power in the years to come.

The external threats posed by Saladin further complicated the situation. The constant threat of Muslim invasion forced the regency to allocate resources towards defense, which further strained already limited resources. The constant threat of invasion often distracted the regency from dealing with the urgent need for effective governance. The competing demands of diplomacy, defense, and internal political conflicts forced the regency council to constantly re-evaluate its priorities, with only a limited capacity for achieving a stable political state. This led to periods of weakness and instability.

Baldwin IV's growing understanding of Saladin's capabilities and intentions, alongside his emerging skill in military strategy, shaped

his approach to governance. He began to actively develop alliances and forge strategic partnerships to mitigate the external threats. While the regency struggled with internal affairs, the young king began to focus on the strategic implications of Saladin's rise,
foreshadowing his later decisive military campaigns. He started to grasp that a strong military was not only a necessity but also a crucial element in maintaining political stability within the realm.

The challenges faced during Baldwin IV's regency period shaped him into a powerful ruler. The experiences of navigating intricate power struggles, dealing with rebellious barons, and managing the threat from Saladin would prove invaluable in his subsequent years as a king. The years spent under the regency served as a formidable training ground, honing his skills as a political strategist and
solidifying his resolve to secure the future of his kingdom. It was in these tumultuous years that he developed the remarkable leadership skills that would later define his reign. The unstable foundation of his early years, marked by the struggles of the regency, only strengthened his resolve and prepared him to face the daunting challenges that lay ahead. The lessons learned in this period of power struggles and external threat would serve him well as he navigated the complex politics and warfare of the Crusader States.

Chapter 6

The Battle of Montgisard, A Triumph Against the Odds

~~Chapter 6~~

The year 1177 witnessed a pivotal moment in the history of the Crusader Kingdom of Jerusalem – the Battle of Montgisard. This clash, pitting the youthful King Baldwin IV against the formidable Saladin, was a David-and-Goliath story played out on the dusty plains of Palestine. Saladin, having consolidated his power in Egypt and Syria, presented an unprecedented threat. His ambition was not merely to conquer isolated Crusader territories, but to erase the Kingdom of Jerusalem entirely, a goal that struck at the very heart of Christendom's presence in the Holy Land. His army, a vast and powerful force drawn from across the Muslim world, dwarfed the Kingdom's relatively small military.

Saladin's campaign began with a calculated strategy. He aimed to exploit the Kingdom's internal divisions, still recovering from the tumultuous regency period and the ongoing power struggles among the nobility. His army moved swiftly, aiming to capture key cities and fortresses before the Kingdom could muster a unified defense.

He swept through the countryside, laying siege to towns, and spreading fear and uncertainty among the populace. The swiftness and decisiveness of Saladin's initial advances sent shock waves through the Kingdom, amplifying anxieties and divisions already present amongst the barons. Many nobles, accustomed to infighting and self-serving ambitions, were slow to react, their concerns more focused on protecting their individual territories than on the collective survival of the Kingdom. This fragmentation hindered the Kingdom's ability to raise a substantial and unified army capable of confronting Saladin's formidable force.

Baldwin IV, however, was not caught unawares. His keen understanding of both military strategy and political maneuvering, honed in the crucible of his years under the regency, proved invaluable in this crisis. He quickly assessed the situation, recognizing that delaying a decisive confrontation would only give Saladin more time to consolidate his gains and further demoralize the Kingdom's defenses. The young king, despite his debilitating illness, demonstrated exceptional leadership by demonstrating courage and inspiring hope in his people. He immediately began preparations for a battle, despite the glaring disparity in the size of the opposing armies.

His approach was characterized by a remarkable combination of daring and pragmatism. Baldwin understood that a direct confrontation with Saladin's numerically superior army on open ground would be suicidal. Instead, he opted for a more strategic approach, carefully selecting the battlefield and leveraging the terrain to his advantage. He chose Montgisard, a strategically advantageous location that offered the potential to offset the Kingdom's numerical disadvantage. The precise location provided natural defensive features that could aid his smaller army, and he skilfully positioned his troops, capitalising on these characteristics to maximise their effectiveness.

The battle itself was a whirlwind of clashing swords and charging horses. Baldwin, despite the limitations imposed by his leprosy, displayed remarkable courage and leadership on the field. He personally led the charge, his presence inspiring his troops and instilling in them a sense of unwavering determination. He didn't simply oversee the battle from afar; his engagement was pivotal in turning the tide of the conflict. Contemporary accounts depict him riding at the forefront of his troops, leading the decisive maneuvers and directing the battle's trajectory with unparalleled bravery.

Accounts portray him as a figure of exceptional strength and resilience, his determination against the odds inspiring his soldiers.

Saladin's army, initially confident in their superior numbers, was taken aback by the ferocity of the Crusader defense and the unexpected tactical brilliance of Baldwin IV's strategy. The King's knowledge of the terrain and his masterful use of it played a critical role in the battle's outcome. The Crusaders, though smaller in number, were highly skilled and well-disciplined. They were deeply committed to defending their homes and faith, and their fighting prowess was a testament to their superior training and their strong will. The chosen battleground significantly hindered Saladin's attempts to exploit his numerical advantage. He couldn't fully deploy his much larger force, limiting its effectiveness and undermining his initial strategic plans.

~~undermining his initial strategic plans.~~

The battle raged for hours. The Crusaders, fighting with the courage born of desperation and inspired by their king's own bravery, inflicted heavy casualties on Saladin's army. Saladin, initially confident of a swift victory, found himself facing an unexpectedly tenacious resistance. The battle was a testament to the Crusaders' skill and determination, highlighting the crucial role of strategic battlefield positioning in military success. The battlefield itself played a key role, restricting Saladin's ability to maneuver his superior numbers effectively.

The clash was not without its critical moments. At several points, the Crusaders appeared to falter under the relentless pressure of Saladin's forces. But each time, Baldwin's leadership and the unwavering commitment of his men prevented a total collapse. He inspired his troops to remain steadfast in the face of adversity, exhibiting incredible stamina and strategic prowess. He repeatedly adapted his tactics as the battle progressed, responding to shifts in momentum and maintaining a strong defense that pushed back against Saladin's offensive surges.

The turning point of the battle came with a daring flanking maneuver executed by Baldwin IV. He personally led a small contingent of knights in a swift attack on Saladin's right flank, surprising the enemy and causing widespread confusion and disruption. This unexpected offensive destabilised the entire army, breaking the momentum of Saladin's attacks and turning the tide of the battle. The attack caught Saladin off guard and caused his lines to falter, leading to a cascade of retreats that threatened to unravel his whole army.

As the day wore on, Saladin's forces, weakened by casualties and demoralized by the tenacity of the Crusader resistance, began to retreat. The battle ended with a decisive Crusader victory, a triumph against overwhelming odds. Saladin's army, though far larger, suffered significant losses, and the initial momentum of his campaign was effectively shattered. The victory at Montgisard not only saved the

Kingdom of Jerusalem from imminent destruction, but it also significantly enhanced Baldwin IV's prestige and military reputation both within the Kingdom and throughout Europe.

The Battle of Montgisard had far-reaching consequences, shaping the course of the Crusader states for years to come. Saladin, though initially setback, remained a formidable opponent. However, the victory at Montgisard demonstrated the effectiveness of skillful leadership and strategic planning, even when confronting an enemy vastly superior in numbers. It highlighted Baldwin IV's military genius and his ability to inspire unwavering loyalty and courage in his soldiers. The victory was a testament to his strategic acumen, his personal bravery, and his remarkable ability to inspire hope in the face of seemingly insurmountable odds.

The aftermath of the battle saw a period of relative peace and stability in the Kingdom, granting Baldwin IV some respite to consolidate his power and address the internal divisions within his kingdom. He used this period to build upon his success, strengthening his alliances and fortifying the kingdom's defenses. The victory had an important psychological impact, significantly bolstering the morale of the Crusaders and deterring Saladin from launching further large-scale offensives for some time.

The Battle of Montgisard remains a powerful symbol of courage, resilience and strategic brilliance. It shows the incredible leadership of King Baldwin IV, a young king afflicted by a devastating disease but endowed with unparalleled strategic and military talents. This momentous battle, a victory snatched from the jaws of defeat, firmly established him as a military leader of exceptional caliber, leaving a legacy in the annals of medieval military history. His triumph at Montgisard not only saved the Kingdom of Jerusalem from immediate annihilation but also cemented his place as one of the most significant figures in the history of the Crusader states. The battle serves as a compelling illustration of how strategic prowess and inspired leadership can overcome seemingly insurmountable obstacles on the battlefield.

The victory achieved at Montgisard stands as a testament to the courage and skill of Baldwin IV and his troops and a critical turning point in the history of the Kingdom of Jerusalem.

Chapter 7

Military Campaigns and Strategic Alliances Defending the Kingdom

The resounding victory at Montgisard, while a pivotal moment, was not an isolated incident in Baldwin IV's reign. His military genius and astute political maneuvering continued to shape the destiny of the Kingdom of Jerusalem throughout his years on the throne. The years following Montgisard saw a period of relative calm, but the threat posed by Saladin remained ever-present. Baldwin, ever vigilant, used this period of peace not for indolence, but for strengthening the Kingdom's defenses and forging crucial strategic alliances. He understood that the survival of the Kingdom depended not solely on military prowess, but also on shrewd diplomacy and the cultivation of strong bonds with neighboring powers.

One of Baldwin's key strategic priorities was strengthening the defenses of the Kingdom's vulnerable borders. He initiated a comprehensive program of fortification, focusing on key strategic locations such as strategically important castles and cities. This involved not only repairs and upgrades to existing structures, but also the construction of new fortifications designed to withstand prolonged sieges. This infrastructural development was not merely a military exercise; it also served as a powerful symbol of the Kingdom's resilience and determination to withstand external threats. The construction efforts employed both local laborers and skilled craftsmen brought in from across the kingdom. The commitment to upgrading the kingdom's defenses demonstrated the king's foresight and his pragmatic understanding of the challenges ahead. The increased fortification created significant obstacles to any potential invasion forces, buying valuable time for the kingdom's army to respond and strategize. Furthermore, the presence of heavily fortified settlements instilled a sense of security among the local population, boosting morale and enhancing the kingdom's overall resilience.

Beyond physical fortifications, Baldwin IV recognized the critical importance of maintaining strong alliances. He skillfully navigated the complex web of relationships between the various Crusader states, constantly striving to foster unity and cooperation against the common enemy. While internal rivalries and disagreements among the nobility posed a persistent challenge, Baldwin worked tirelessly to reconcile factions, promoting a sense of shared purpose and understanding among the different groups within the kingdom.

He utilized a combination of diplomatic negotiations and skillful political maneuvering to consolidate his support among the powerful lords and knights of his kingdom. The success of this strategy was evident in the improved coordination and collaboration among Crusader forces in subsequent military engagements.

The Kingdom's relationship with the Byzantine Empire, though often fraught with tension, proved crucial during this period.

Baldwin understood the strategic value of an alliance with Byzantium, particularly in countering Saladin's growing influence. He pursued diplomatic initiatives aimed at improving relations and securing Byzantine support, employing skillful diplomacy to address the historical animosities and competing interests between the two kingdoms. While past conflicts and mistrust cast a long shadow, Baldwin recognized the benefits of a united front against a common enemy. He engaged in correspondence with the Byzantine Emperor, highlighting their shared interests in maintaining a Christian presence in the Levant. This diplomatic engagement involved negotiations to resolve outstanding disputes and to establish a firm basis for cooperation. The alliance proved valuable in sharing intelligence and coordinating military efforts, allowing the Crusader states to counter Saladin's advancements with increased efficiency.

Beyond Byzantium, Baldwin IV also cultivated alliances with other regional powers. He understood the need to maintain diplomatic contact with various factions and states, often playing these alliances against each other to maintain a strategic balance of power. He engaged in negotiations to secure military aid and financial resources from European powers, ensuring that the Kingdom of Jerusalem retained access to external support whenever needed. This deft balancing act was critical in maintaining the Kingdom's stability and providing a buffer against potential threats from various directions.

While diplomatic efforts played a critical role in the Kingdom's defense, military campaigns remained essential. Baldwin IV's military strategy was marked by a careful blend of offensive and defensive maneuvers, tailored to the specific circumstances of each engagement. He understood the importance of choosing appropriate battlefields, using superior tactical skills and effectively employing his troops. His leadership inspired his knights and soldiers, leading to impressive victories even in the face of superior numbers. He avoided major confrontations unless the strategic conditions were favorable, instead opting for smaller-scale engagements to wear down his opponents and conserve his forces. His tactical decisions prioritized the protection of vital infrastructure and the security of the kingdom's population.

Several key military engagements showed Baldwin's skills. These were not necessarily large-scale battles like Montgisard, but rather strategic campaigns carefully designed to disrupt Saladin's plans and inflict significant losses. These operations often involved swiftly targeting vulnerable supply lines, ambushing smaller enemy detachments, or defending key strategic strongholds. Baldwin IV utilized both his own highly trained troops, supplemented by contingents of allies from neighboring Crusader States. This demonstrates a solid understanding of resource management and the importance of strategic alliances. The successful implementation of these strategies demonstrated Baldwin's leadership and resourcefulness.

For example, in 1179, Baldwin successfully repelled an attack on the strategically important city of Ascalon, demonstrating his ability to coordinate his forces effectively and repel an aggressive Saladin assault. This victory underscores the significance of effective leadership and timely military interventions in safeguarding vital infrastructure and resources. The defense of Ascalon prevented Saladin from establishing a stronger foothold on the coastal plain, limiting his capacity to disrupt crucial trade routes and threatening important Crusader strongholds. This triumph underscores Baldwin's ability to anticipate enemy strategies, prepare for defensive operations and inspire unwavering loyalty amongst his troops.

Another example is his careful defense of the southern borders of the Kingdom. Recognizing the vulnerability of this region to raids from Egypt, Baldwin implemented a strategy of establishing fortified outposts and strategically positioning his troops to counter these incursions. This demonstrated Baldwin's deep understanding of defensive warfare, preventing Saladin from exploiting the southern region's weaknesses. These tactical positions, combined with swift counter-offensives, effectively deterred larger-scale incursions and minimized the damage caused by smaller raids. His focus on strategic defense and careful planning helped to preserve crucial infrastructure, resources, and the overall stability of the Kingdom.

Baldwin IV's reign, despite its tragic brevity, stands as a testament to the power of strategic brilliance and inspired leadership. His military campaigns and diplomatic maneuvers were not merely acts of defense, but proactive measures to ensure the survival and prosperity of the Kingdom of Jerusalem. He understood that the Kingdom's survival depended on a sophisticated interplay of military might and political acumen, a combination that he masterfully employed throughout his reign. Even while battling a debilitating disease, his dedication to his Kingdom ensured his place in history as one of the most remarkable and effective rulers of the Crusader States. His legacy extended beyond the battlefield; his strategic vision shaped the Kingdom's political landscape and military capabilities, leaving a profound impact long after his untimely death. His ability to inspire loyalty, coordinate alliances and achieve strategic victories against formidable foes ensured his enduring legacy. The success of his strategies and the lasting stability he provided highlights his extraordinary leadership and unwavering dedication to the Kingdom of Jerusalem. His reign serves as a compelling case study in the complex interplay between military prowess, diplomatic skill, and the unwavering resolve of a leader determined to defend his kingdom against seemingly insurmountable odds.

Chapter 8

Military Innovations and Tactics Adapting to the Challenges

The effectiveness of Baldwin IV's military leadership stemmed not only from his inherent strategic brilliance but also from his willingness to adapt and innovate. The Crusader states faced a unique set of challenges, demanding flexibility that went beyond the traditional European methods of warfare. Saladin's army, for example, employed different tactics and weaponry, necessitating a corresponding evolution in Crusader strategies. Baldwin IV recognized this need and actively sought to improve his army's capabilities.

One of Baldwin's most significant contributions was the refinement of castle defense. While the construction of new fortifications was crucial, he also recognized the importance of improving existing defenses. He introduced innovative techniques in siege warfare, incorporating new defensive measures into older castles. These improvements often involved the reinforcement of walls, the installation of improved siege engines (like mangonels and trebuchets), and the strategic placement of defensive towers and outposts. He understood that strong defense wasn't just about brute strength, but also about employing clever tactics and utilizing the terrain to maximize defensive capabilities. His focus extended beyond the physical structures; he implemented improved training regimens for garrison troops, emphasizing the importance of coordinated defense and efficient resource management within the castles themselves. These improvements were not limited to large, strategically significant castles; Baldwin also invested in upgrading the defenses of smaller border fortifications, recognizing their vital role in hindering enemy incursions and preventing widespread raids. This comprehensive approach to castle defense formed a crucial element of his overall military strategy.

Furthermore, Baldwin IV understood the importance of adapting to the changing nature of warfare. Saladin's forces were renowned for their cavalry, skilled in rapid maneuvers and flanking attacks. To counter this, Baldwin IV began to incorporate new tactics into his army's repertoire. He focused on improving the mobility and maneuverability of his own cavalry, emphasizing swift responses and coordinated movements to match Saladin's capabilities. This involved rigorous training that honed the knights' ability to swiftly regroup and counter enemy charges. He also recognized the value of strategic retreats and carefully planned ambushes. Instead of always engaging in direct confrontations, he used tactical withdrawals to lure the enemy into unfavorable terrain, or to exhaust their resources before striking a decisive blow. This pragmatic approach, prioritizing strategic gains over outright battles, distinguished his military style.

The utilization of intelligence was another key aspect of Baldwin IV's military innovation. He established a sophisticated intelligence network to gather information on Saladin's movements, strategies, and troop deployments. This network tapped into both local informants and diplomatic channels, providing timely warnings and allowing for preemptive measures. Baldwin understood that military success was as much dependent on intelligence as on brute force. This network was instrumental in allowing him to anticipate Saladin's actions, and therefore effectively utilize his resources to counter threats before they fully materialized. This ability to anticipate enemy movements and prepare effective counter-strategies formed a central tenet of Baldwin's successful military campaigns.

Moreover, Baldwin IV's military innovations went beyond tactics and strategy. He actively sought to improve the equipment and weaponry of his army. While the Crusader armies were largely reliant on the heavy cavalry, he also recognized the importance of supplementing these forces with lighter, more mobile troops. He incorporated a greater number of light infantries, and increasingly utilized archers in his army, demonstrating an understanding of the effectiveness of combined arms warfare. These lighter troops could act as scouts, harass enemy movements, and protect the flanks of the main army. The archers, especially, proved effective in countering the cavalry charges, providing much-needed support to the heavily armored knights. This diversification of his forces mirrored his strategic flexibility. He understood the importance of adaptability and tailoring his military responses to the specific challenges presented by the adversary. This strategic blend of troops proved essential to counter Saladin's diverse military _capabilities.

The logistics of supplying and supporting a Crusader army were also a key concern. Baldwin IV implemented improvements in the army's supply chains, improving efficiency in moving provisions and ensuring the army was well-supplied even during prolonged campaigns. This aspect, frequently overlooked, was a cornerstone of his success, as prolonged sieges or protracted campaigns required meticulous planning and effective resource management. He established improved communication networks, allowing for the coordination of supply routes and the rapid transmission of vital information to units stationed at great distances.

Furthermore, Baldwin IV's strategic thinking extended beyond the immediate battlefield. He understood that the long-term success of the Kingdom of Jerusalem depended on maintaining a strong economy and a stable society. He therefore implemented policies that strengthened the kingdom's infrastructure, fostering trade and encouraging agricultural production. This understanding that military might wasn't solely about soldiers and weapons, but relied heavily on a supporting infrastructure, indicates a broad and forward-looking approach to strategic planning. A healthy and prosperous kingdom could better support its military, making it more sustainable and effective over time.

Baldwin IV's military innovations were not merely isolated changes but a coherent system of adaptations and improvements, tailored to the specific challenges posed by Saladin and the changing dynamics of warfare in the Levant. He consistently sought to improve his army's capabilities, adapt its tactics to counter evolving threats, and ensure its efficient supply and support. His understanding that military strength was only one facet of the Kingdom's survival, also recognizing the importance of internal stability and economic growth, demonstrated a comprehensive and strategic vision that went beyond immediate military concerns. He demonstrated an unparalleled adaptability, constantly refining his approach in response to the evolving situation, a defining characteristic of his remarkable leadership. His reign showcases a masterful combination of strategic vision, tactical innovation, and a profound understanding of the interplay between military strength, economic

stability, and effective governance. It is this holistic approach that solidified his place as one of the most brilliant military leaders of the Crusader States. His legacy extends far beyond individual victories, representing a significant contribution to the evolution of military strategy within the context of the Crusades. His innovations and adaptations continue to be studied by military historians, offering valuable insights into the challenges of medieval warfare and the importance of adaptability and strategic thinking.

Chapter 9

The Role of the Military Orders Knights Templar and Hospitallers

The success of Baldwin IV's military campaigns was inextricably linked to the performance of the powerful military orders operating within the Kingdom of Jerusalem: The Knights Templar and the Hospitallers. These monastic orders, sworn to poverty, chastity, and obedience, were also formidable fighting forces, possessing significant military resources and expertise. Their relationship with Baldwin IV was complex, characterized by periods of close cooperation and moments of tension, reflecting the inherent power dynamics between a secular ruler and immensely wealthy and influential religious organizations.

The Knights Templar, officially known as the Poor Fellow-Soldiers of Christ and of the Temple of Solomon, were renowned for their highly disciplined and heavily armored cavalry. Their wealth, accumulated through donations and land holdings throughout Europe and the Levant, enabled them to equip themselves with the finest arms and armor, making them a crucial component of Baldwin IV's military strength. Their centralized organization, with a Grand Master at its head, allowed for swift mobilization and coordination, features that Baldwin IV deftly leveraged. The Templars often formed the vanguard of Baldwin's armies, their imposing presence breaking enemy lines and providing a solid anchor for the rest of the Crusader forces. Their battlefield prowess was considerable, honed through years of experience fighting in the volatile conditions of the Levant. Baldwin skillfully integrated their strengths into his overall strategy, often employing them in decisive actions that tipped the balance in his favor. He understood their value not just as shock troops, but also as highly trained scouts and for the intelligence they could gather from their widespread networks of contacts across the region. The Templar network, with its holdings in key locations, acted as a vital component of the Kingdom's intelligence apparatus, providing early warning of Saladin's movements and intentions.

However, the relationship between Baldwin and the Templars wasn't always without friction. The Templars' considerable wealth and power occasionally leads to disagreements over strategy and resources. The Order possessed its own independent command structure, and while generally loyal to the King, there were instances where their independent actions or priorities might conflict with Baldwin IV's overall plans. Their loyalty was ultimately to their Grand Master and to their own religious mission; this created a delicate balance between the needs of the Kingdom and the interests of the Order. This tension was particularly evident during periods of political instability, where the Order might seek to safeguard its own interests even if that meant deviating from the King's explicit orders. Baldwin, however, was a shrewd ruler; he understood the potential dangers of alienating such a powerful force, carefully balancing cooperation and control to maintain a constructive relationship.

The Hospitallers, officially known as the Knights Hospitaller of the Order of St. John of Jerusalem, were similarly vital to Baldwin IV's military success. Originally founded as a charitable order to care for pilgrims, the Hospitallers also evolved into a powerful military force. They, too, possessed considerable wealth and manpower, and their expertise in both battlefield combat and medical care made them an invaluable asset. They controlled strategic locations and, like the Templars, established a network of fortifications and connections that provided Baldwin with crucial intelligence. Unlike the Templars who focused almost exclusively on mounted warfare, the Hospitallers maintained a more diverse force, including a substantial contingent of infantry, which proved useful in siege warfare and in providing support for the heavier cavalry. This diversity in their military composition complemented the Templars' strengths, contributing to the overall tactical versatility of Baldwin's armies.

The Hospitallers, however, often played a more ambivalent role in the political landscape than the Templars. Their commitment to the defense of the Kingdom was undoubtedly strong, but their extensive network of hospitals and their concern for pilgrims sometimes placed them in a position of mediating between different factions, potentially creating tensions with the King. This mediating role, while beneficial in some cases for maintaining stability, could sometimes be viewed by Baldwin IV as a form of independent maneuvering. Balancing the Hospitallers' need for independence in their charitable work with their military obligations to the Crown presented a significant challenge for Baldwin. He managed this delicate balancing act, though, using diplomacy and a nuanced understanding of their priorities, successfully integrating their considerable resources and capabilities into his military plans.

The cooperation between Baldwin IV, the Templars, and the Hospitallers was not always seamless; navigating the power dynamics between a secular monarchy and powerful religious military orders was a constant challenge. Strategic disagreements occasionally arose, particularly concerning resource allocation, command structures, and the overall direction of military operations. The immense wealth and power of the orders sometimes presented a potential threat to royal authority; however, Baldwin IV skillfully managed these tensions. He recognized the importance of these orders, understanding their critical contributions to the Kingdom's defense, and deftly leveraged their resources while maintaining his own authority.

Baldwin IV's strategic brilliance was displayed not only in his battlefield tactics but also in his skillful management of relationships with the military orders. He understood the need for a balance between strong leadership and effective collaboration. He maintained close ties with the leadership of both orders, ensuring that they remained aligned with his strategic objectives, while at the same time avoiding a complete dependence on them. This prevented the orders from wielding undue political influence and safeguarding his own sovereign power. He cleverly utilized their vast networks for intelligence gathering, strategic positioning, and military reinforcement, seamlessly incorporating their strengths into his wider military strategies.

The success of Baldwin IV's military campaigns was demonstrably reliant on his understanding of the military orders, and his ability to utilize them effectively. His skillful diplomacy, strategic insight, and pragmatic approach to power enabled him to maintain a functional, if occasionally strained, partnership with the Templars and the Hospitallers. Their combined strength was a key element in his remarkable victories against Saladin and the Ayyubid forces. The detailed coordination between the royal army and these orders demonstrates a level of organizational prowess and understanding that was relatively unique in the chaotic political and military environment of the 12th century Levant. Their cooperation, and Baldwin's management thereof, formed a fundamental pillar of the Kingdom's defensive capabilities, prolonging its existence against considerable odds. The study of these complex relationships offers important insights into the political and military dynamics of the Crusader states, and how a ruler could strategically leverage religious and military institutions to achieve a greater objective.

Baldwin IV's legacy is not solely confined to his own military genius, but also encompasses his ability to forge, maintain, and harness the power of these influential religious military orders to the benefit of his kingdom. The nuanced relationship he fostered with these potent forces was, in essence, a testament to his overall strategic thinking and political acumen, as much as his battlefield successes. It was this intricate interplay of power and cooperation that ultimately allowed the Kingdom of Jerusalem to resist its enemies for so long, even in the face of a formidable adversary like Saladin. Understanding this relationship is key to understanding the complexities of the Kingdom of Jerusalem and the reign of its remarkable King.

Chapter 10

Maintaining Order Amidst Conflict Securing Internal Stability

Maintaining internal stability within the Kingdom of Jerusalem during Baldwin IV's reign presented a formidable challenge, intricately interwoven with the ongoing external conflicts against Saladin and his Ayyubid forces. The king's success in navigating these turbulent waters stemmed from a multifaceted approach that involved shrewd political maneuvering, effective judicial systems, and a deft handling of the various factions vying for power within his realm.

One of Baldwin's key strategies was to foster a sense of shared purpose among the diverse populace of the Kingdom. This wasn't a homogenous society; it comprised Franks, Armenians, Greeks, Syrians, and many other ethnic and religious groups, each with its own customs, traditions, and often conflicting interests. Baldwin understood that a unified front was crucial against external threats and actively sought to cultivate a sense of collective identity, emphasizing their shared role in defending the Kingdom against its enemies. This was achieved not through forced assimilation but through a pragmatic approach of recognizing and respecting the unique identities of various groups while emphasizing their common goals. He encouraged cooperation between different communities through shared projects, such as fortification repairs, the organization of local militias, and the joint administration of vital resources like water rights. This fostered a sense of shared investment in the Kingdom's well-being, promoting cooperation and reducing inter-communal friction.

Beyond fostering a sense of shared purpose, Baldwin IV implemented robust judicial mechanisms to address internal conflict. The Kingdom of Jerusalem had a sophisticated legal system, drawing on both Roman and canon law, which helped to provide a framework for resolving disputes between individuals and groups. Baldwin ensured the fair and impartial application of the law, regardless of the social status or religious affiliation of the parties involved. This was crucial for maintaining social order and preventing conflicts from escalating into larger-scale violence. He appointed highly qualified judges and officials to administer justice,

often selecting individuals known for their integrity and impartiality, regardless of their background. This demonstrably contributed to public confidence in the judicial system and helped to prevent the rise of private vendettas or extrajudicial settlements that could destabilize the Kingdom. This commitment to the rule of law strengthened the legitimacy of Baldwin's rule, bolstering his authority and reducing the likelihood of internal rebellion.

Furthermore, the King's skillful handling of the powerful barons, who held considerable influence and often clashed over territories, resources, and power, was essential for maintaining internal stability. The feudal system, while beneficial for the defense of the Kingdom, also engendered conflicts between powerful lords, each vying for influence and dominance. Baldwin recognized this inherent instability and addressed it with diplomacy and strategic alliances. He fostered loyal relationships with key barons through careful patronage, strategic marriages, and a commitment to the fair application of feudal law. He avoided provoking open conflict, and whenever disagreements arose, he attempted to resolve them through mediation, negotiation, and compromise, demonstrating fairness and impartiality to maintain balance of power. He

meticulously appointed officials and advisors who could both effectively administer, and judge based on an established, fair legal framework. This prevented the escalation of petty rivalries into widespread conflicts that could easily distract from the fight against external enemies. His understanding of the delicate balance between rewarding loyalty and maintaining his own sovereign authority was crucial to managing potential conflicts effectively.

The succession issue became a particularly challenging element of internal stability during Baldwin's reign. His illness, which progressively worsened, cast a long shadow over the future of the Kingdom, inviting political maneuvering and potential conflicts. The lack of a clear heir and the conflicting claims of various nobles created fertile ground for potential conflicts and conspiracies.

Baldwin IV, aware of this vulnerability, attempted to carefully manage the succession crisis. He tried several approaches, including designating his nephew, Baldwin of Montferrat, as his heir, and later considering other candidates. His attempts to navigate the succession crisis, however, were often undermined by the ambitions of powerful nobles and the intrigues of his court. The inherent uncertainty surrounding the succession created an unstable environment, fueling speculation and potentially encouraging opportunistic actions by those eager to secure power for themselves.

This constant threat of internal conflict added to the challenges Baldwin faced in defending the Kingdom from external enemies. The delicate balance between the need to appoint a successor and the fear of provoking conflict required astute political judgment and a capacity for deft diplomacy, all of which were hallmarks of his reign.
The economic situation also played a significant role in the maintenance of internal stability. The Kingdom of Jerusalem, despite its strategic location and trade routes, faced consistent economic challenges. The continuous wars against the Ayyubids placed a heavy burden on the royal treasury. Baldwin's fiscal policies played a pivotal role in mitigating this financial burden. He implemented measures to improve tax collection, streamlining the system to reduce waste and fraud and to ensure greater efficiency and accountability. This strengthened the royal finances, enabling him to better equip his army, invest in fortifications, and maintain essential public services. He also actively sought to promote trade and commerce, encouraging the development of urban centers and fostering relations with trading partners in the East and West. A stable economy provided a more stable social order, lessening the likelihood of widespread unrest arising from poverty or economic inequality. The king's pragmatic management of the Kingdom's economy was crucial in maintaining internal stability and ensuring the resources were available for military campaigns and civil
administration.

In summary, Baldwin IV's success in maintaining internal stability during his reign was a testament to his political acumen, his understanding of the various factions within his Kingdom, and his capacity for astute diplomacy and decisive action. His ability to navigate the intricacies of feudal politics, manage conflicts among powerful barons, address economic challenges, and maintain a robust judicial system were all crucial to preserving the unity and stability of the Kingdom of Jerusalem, despite the relentless pressure from external threats. His efforts to create a sense of shared purpose and identity, combined with his strong leadership and commitment to justice, enabled him to maintain a relative equilibrium within his realm, allowing him to focus his military strength on resisting the Ayyubid threat. The internal stability he fostered, therefore, wasn't just a passive state but an active achievement, a critical element contributing to the remarkable resilience of the Kingdom under his rule. His reign highlights the fact that military strength alone was insufficient; effective governance and internal cohesion were essential pillars of the Kingdom's survival in a time of constant war and political turmoil. The intricacies of balancing these internal and external pressures reveal the complexity of leadership in the Crusader states and the extraordinary skills required to sustain a kingdom on the volatile frontiers of the medieval world.

Chapter 11

Raynald of Chatillon, A Dangerous Ally

Raynald of Chatillon represented a particularly thorny problem for Baldwin IV. While ostensibly an ally, the lord of Kerak possessed a personality and ambitions that frequently threatened the fragile peace Baldwin worked so hard to maintain. Raynald's acquisition of the strategically important Transjordanian fortress of Kerak, a prize won through marriage, positioned him as a significant power broker in the region, but also as a constant source of friction. His relentless raiding activities against Muslim caravans and settlements, far from being a peripheral concern, significantly escalated tensions with Saladin and undermined Baldwin's delicate attempts at diplomacy and limited truces. This was not simply a matter of individual banditry; it was a deeply destabilizing factor that had far-reaching geopolitical consequences for the entire kingdom.

The contrast between Baldwin's cautious and diplomatic approach to conflict resolution and Raynald's aggressive, almost reckless, belligerence was stark. Baldwin understood that the Kingdom of Jerusalem, perpetually under threat from powerful neighbors, could not afford to engage in protracted conflicts on multiple fronts. His strategic focus was on maintaining a balance of power, carefully choosing his battles and seeking secure alliances wherever possible. Raynald, however, seemed driven by personal ambition and a thirst for plunder, seemingly unconcerned about the broader implications of his actions. His raids, while lucrative for him, served as potent provocations, often prompting retaliatory actions from Saladin that threatened to unravel any fragile diplomatic arrangements Baldwin had painstakingly constructed.

The nature of feudal relationships within the Crusader states further complicated the situation. While Baldwin held ultimate authority as

King, his power was not absolute. The powerful lords, like Raynald, possessed considerable autonomy and often acted according to their own interests, sometimes in defiance of royal authority. Attempting to directly control Raynald's actions would risk open rebellion, undermining the stability Baldwin sought to preserve. Thus,

Baldwin faced a dilemma: he needed to restrain Raynald without provoking a major conflict within his own kingdom. This required a delicate balancing act, a continual negotiation between maintaining the uneasy peace and responding to the increasingly aggressive actions of Raynald.

The geographical location of Kerak itself further exacerbated the problem. Situated in Transjordan, Kerak controlled vital trade routes and served as a strategic base for raids against Muslim territories. Its remoteness, however, made it difficult for Baldwin to directly supervise or control Raynald's activities. While Baldwin possessed a strong standing army, deploying those troops to restrain Raynald would divert crucial resources away from other vital defense efforts and potentially weaken the kingdom's defenses against a larger-scale invasion. The cost-benefit calculation was consistently skewed in favor of avoiding open conflict with one of his vassals.

Furthermore, the religious dimension of the conflict added another layer of complexity. Raynald's actions against Muslims were often portrayed as acts of religious fervor, even if driven primarily by personal ambition. This religious justification complicated Baldwin's attempts to mediate or control Raynald's behavior. Any perceived leniency towards Raynald could be interpreted as weakness or compromise by the Frankish community, and any punitive action might embolden the Muslim enemies, especially Saladin, who eagerly sought justification for his own aggressive actions. This intricate interplay of political and religious factors added another dimension to the challenge Baldwin faced.

Beyond the immediate military and political consequences, Raynald's actions also had profound economic ramifications for the kingdom. While the short-term gains from plunder were undoubtedly tempting for Raynald and his men, the long-term effects were decidedly negative. Raynald's raids disrupted trade routes, hindering the flow of goods and harming the economy of the kingdom. Furthermore, they fueled resentment amongst the Muslim population, potentially destabilizing the fragile truce between the kingdom and its neighbors. This economic instability threatened to undermine the very foundations of the kingdom, adding yet another layer to the complex challenges facing Baldwin.

The issue of Raynald's actions also highlighted the inherent tensions within the Crusader states. The Kingdom of Jerusalem was a complex entity, comprising diverse groups with often-conflicting interests. While Raynald was ostensibly a loyal vassal, his actions consistently challenged the king's authority and threatened the stability of the kingdom. Baldwin's struggles to contain Raynald revealed the limitations of royal power within the feudal structure of the Crusader states and the difficulty of enforcing central authority in a fragmented geopolitical landscape. The internal struggle between a king seeking to maintain peace and a powerful vassal seeking personal glory underscores the inherently unstable nature of the Crusader kingdoms.

Baldwin's attempts to manage the situation with Raynald were marked by a series of subtle and often unsuccessful attempts to guide or restrain the lord of Kerak. He used diplomatic means, personal appeals, and carefully crafted letters, but Raynald, seemingly emboldened by his strategic position and the difficulty of controlling him, largely ignored these attempts. Baldwin's own health deteriorated during these years, further weakening his ability to exert firm control over his unruly vassal. The increasing frequency of Raynald's provocative actions suggests an almost deliberate disregard for the King's authority, indicating a fundamental clash of personalities and priorities.

The escalating tensions between Raynald and Saladin, largely fueled by Raynald's raids, contributed significantly to the deterioration of relations between the Kingdom and its Muslim neighbors. Saladin, increasingly frustrated by Raynald's provocations and Baldwin's seemingly ineffectual attempts at restraint, began to see the kingdom as a whole as a potential target. Raynald's actions, therefore, unintentionally shifted Saladin's focus from localized skirmishes to considering a more wide-ranging campaign against the kingdom itself. The cumulative impact of these raids significantly eroded the possibility of long-term peace, making future conflict almost inevitable.

In conclusion, Raynald of Chatillon presents a fascinating case study in the complexities of power and relationships within the Crusader states. His relationship with Baldwin IV was one of uneasy alliance, marked by a constant tension between royal authority and the ambitions of a powerful lord. Raynald's actions, driven by personal ambition and a disregard for the kingdom's overall stability, ultimately contributed to the escalating conflict with Saladin and the destabilization of the kingdom. Baldwin's attempts to manage this relationship highlight the limitations of royal power within the feudal system and the inherent challenges of governing a diverse and geographically dispersed kingdom under constant external threat. The story of Raynald's actions serves as a reminder of the precarious balance of power in the Crusader states and the multifaceted challenges faced by Baldwin IV in his efforts to secure the survival of his kingdom. His failure to fully restrain Raynald serves as a significant contributing factor to the eventual downfall of the kingdom, a reminder that even the most capable ruler can be undermined by the actions of a powerful and rebellious vassal. The constant tension between internal stability and external threats, epitomized by the relationship between Baldwin and Raynald, ultimately shaped the fate of the Crusader states.

Chapter 12

Sibylla and Guy de Lusignan A Threat to the Throne

The shadow of Raynald of Chatillon's disruptive actions loomed large, but the internal threat to Baldwin IV's reign proved equally, if not more, perilous. This stemmed from the volatile relationship between the king and his sister, Sibylla, and her increasingly powerful husband, Guy de Lusignan. Sibylla, as Baldwin's sister and a direct heir, held a significant position within the complex web of power dynamics within the kingdom. Her marriage, however, significantly altered this equation. Guy, initially lacking significant territorial holdings or a powerful family backing within the kingdom, rose rapidly in influence, largely due to his marriage to the princess. This ascent was a source of considerable concern for Baldwin, who acutely understood the potential ramifications of such a rapid elevation in power.

Baldwin's anxieties were not unfounded. The Crusader kingdoms were founded on a complex interplay of feudal loyalties, religious zeal, and political maneuvering. While Baldwin's kingship was undeniably powerful, it rested upon the delicate balance of power amongst the various noble families and their conflicting ambitions.

The elevation of Guy de Lusignan, a relatively newcomer to the intricate political landscape, threatened to disrupt this precariously balanced system.

Guy de Lusignan's personality and ambitions contrasted sharply with Baldwin's cautious pragmatism. While Baldwin emphasized diplomacy and strategic alliances, Guy was perceived as more impulsive and less politically astute. This difference in temperament and political approach created a significant chasm between the king and his brother-in-law, fueling concerns about Guy's fitness to rule. Baldwin, ever the astute strategist, likely foresaw the potential for Guy to mismanage the kingdom's delicate political relationships, potentially sparking conflicts with neighboring powers.

The concerns regarding Guy's capacity to rule went beyond mere personality traits. His relatively humble origins within the context of the aristocratic Crusader society created a significant hurdle for his acceptance among the kingdom's powerful nobles. Many of the barons felt that Guy, lacking the established lineage and territorial holdings of the other potential heirs, lacked the legitimacy required to lead the kingdom. This inherent lack of established power base made him vulnerable to manipulation and potentially undermined the authority of the throne. This was a serious consideration for Baldwin, as a weak king would inevitably weaken the kingdom, leaving it vulnerable to external threats.

Furthermore, Guy's rapid accumulation of power and influence through his marriage to Sibylla ignited intense jealousy and resentment among other powerful noble families. This fueled court intrigue and conspiracies against both Sibylla and Guy, exacerbating the already precarious situation. Their very success in ascending the political hierarchy attracted numerous detractors, who saw their rise as an unwarranted intrusion into the established order.

Sibylla, initially seemingly content to support Guy's ambitions, may have found herself caught in a web of her own making. Her unwavering loyalty to her husband, while demonstrating her affection and trust, could have also blinded her to the political realities and the potential ramifications of their growing influence. Her powerful position within the royal family, combined with Guy's rising influence, placed both as central figures in the unfolding drama of succession.

Baldwin's efforts to address this potential crisis were complicated by several factors. His own deteriorating health, stemming from his worsening leprosy, progressively weakened his capacity to directly influence the succession. This left him vulnerable to the machinations of the court and reduced his ability to fully control the events unfolding around him. His attempts to influence the succession through various means—subtle political maneuvering, alliances with other powerful noble families, and even attempts to ensure a different succession route—were constantly challenged by the ever-growing power of Guy and Sibylla.

The situation is further complicated as Baldwin considered alternative succession plans. He explored the possibility of naming a different heir, one who might have better credentials and broader support among the kingdom's nobility, to prevent the potential instability of Guy's ascension to the throne. This, however, would inevitably generate conflict within the royal family and among the barons, potentially resulting in a destabilizing power struggle. The king found himself trapped in a dilemma: maintaining Sibylla's rights as his heir versus ensuring the kingdom's continued stability.

The interplay of religious and secular interests further complicated the issue. The Church, a powerful institution within the Crusader states, held significant sway over matters of succession. Gaining the Church's support was crucial, yet the Church's stance on Guy's suitability to rule was far from certain. Some church leaders may have harbored reservations about Guy's suitability, adding another layer to the already intricate political tapestry.

The struggle for succession wasn't confined to the royal family; it extended to the wider nobility. Powerful noble houses, with their own ambitions and rivalries, became entangled in the unfolding power play. Alliances shifted, betrayals occurred, and the court became a stage for intricate political games, with various factions vying for power and influence. Baldwin, already burdened by his illness and the threats from external enemies, was forced to navigate this labyrinthine political landscape, trying to maintain control amidst this storm of intrigue and competing ambitions.

The looming threat of Saladin further amplified the stakes. The unstable political situation within the kingdom could easily have been exploited by Saladin, weakening the kingdom and potentially jeopardizing its very survival. Baldwin understood this acutely; the internal conflict threatened to overshadow the external threat. He needed to secure the stability of the kingdom, and any dispute over succession risked opening a dangerous internal rift.

Baldwin's attempts to address these challenges were marked by a combination of political maneuvering, strategic alliances, and calculated compromises. He sought to secure the loyalty of key nobles and maintain a semblance of control within the turbulent court, but the relentless pressure of both internal and external threats was overwhelming. The struggle between Baldwin's attempt to maintain a stable succession and the ambition of Sibylla and Guy de Lusignan became one of the defining features of his later reign.

The deteriorating health of Baldwin IV was a crucial factor in the increasing tensions. His weakened state diminished his ability to effectively control the ambitions of Sibylla and Guy. His efforts to navigate the complex political landscape were hampered by the encroaching shadow of his illness and his inability to fully exert his authority. The ensuing power vacuum exacerbated the rivalries within the kingdom, leaving him vulnerable to manipulation.

The story of Baldwin's relationship with Sibylla and Guy de Lusignan is a tragic tale of ambition, betrayal, and the precariousness of power. It encapsulates the complexities of the Crusader kingdoms, where religious fervor, political intrigue, and personal ambitions intertwined to shape the destiny of the kingdom.

The unfolding events highlight the crucial role that family relationships played in the power dynamics of the Crusader states, and how these relationships could dramatically influence the course of history. It serves as a profound illustration of the delicate balance of power in medieval society and the often-fatal consequences of unchecked ambition. The king's struggles with his own family became a microcosm of the larger conflict playing out within the kingdom – a constant struggle for power between competing factions, both within and without the royal family, all set against the backdrop of relentless conflict with their Muslim neighbors.

Baldwin's tragic reign, ultimately cut short by his illness, underscores the fragility of the Crusader kingdoms and the formidable challenges faced by even the most capable of rulers. The unresolved succession issue, ultimately resolved in a way that proved disastrous for the kingdom, demonstrates the far-reaching consequences of the political battles that unfolded during Baldwin's reign and their lasting impact on the fate of the Crusader states.

Chapter 13

The Role of Advisors and Ministers Navigating Political Intrigue

The intricate web of power surrounding Baldwin IV extended far beyond his immediate family. His reign was significantly shaped by the actions and advice, both wise and treacherous, of his advisors and ministers. These individuals, drawn from diverse backgrounds and loyalties, navigated the treacherous currents of court politics, their influence often exceeding their formal titles. Understanding their roles is crucial to grasping the complexities of Baldwin's rule and the ultimate unraveling of his carefully constructed power balance.

Among the most prominent figures in Baldwin's court was Aimery of Lusignan, Guy's older brother. While initially seemingly supportive of the king, Aimery's ambitions and loyalty were always subject to question. He held a significant military command, giving him considerable influence over the kingdom's armed forces, a power he could easily use to further his own, or his brother's, agenda. His actions are often interpreted through the lens of self-preservation and familial loyalty, making it difficult to ascertain the true extent of his support for or opposition to Baldwin IV.

Historians debate whether Aimery was a genuine advisor seeking to serve the kingdom or a cunning opportunist who strategically maneuvered to advance the Lusignan family's interests. His position within the army allowed him to subtly influence troop movements, military strategies, and even the allocation of resources, all of which could be used to advance his family's ambitions.

The Patriarch of Jerusalem, Heraclius, also played a significant, though often ambiguous, role. The Patriarch held immense religious authority, wielding considerable influence over public opinion and the loyalty of the populace. Heraclius's relationship with Baldwin IV was complex, marked by periods of cooperation and conflict. While the king generally respected the Church's authority, their alignment on political matters was often tenuous, particularly when the Patriarch's actions seemed to benefit certain noble families, namely those who opposed Guy de Lusignan. His influence stretched beyond the purely religious; he held significant political power and access to information, capable of subtly shifting the balance of power within the kingdom. Did Heraclius genuinely seek to serve the best interests of the Kingdom, or did his actions betray personal biases and loyalties? The historical record leaves this question open to interpretation.

Another key player was Joscelin III of Edessa, a veteran Crusader leader. A seasoned warrior, Joscelin offered invaluable military counsel and possessed extensive experience in managing the complex dynamics of the Crusader states. He provided a counterbalance to the more impetuous advisors, often advocating for cautious pragmatism and a strong military posture, even as Baldwin IV's health declined. However, Joscelin's advice was not always heeded, and the king's attempts to balance competing opinions often led to a paralysis of decision-making. His military expertise made him a valued asset to Baldwin, but his own ambitions and family connections potentially influenced his advice.

The intricacies of the court extended to those with less overtly powerful positions. The numerous lesser barons and officials, with their fluctuating allegiances, added another layer of complexity to the political landscape. These individuals, often caught between the competing factions of the court, shaped the political environment through their networks and alliances. Their support, or lack thereof, could tip the balance of power in favor of or against certain factions. Their influences were often subtle, operating through whispers, rumors, and carefully orchestrated alliances.

Analyzing the effectiveness of Baldwin's advisors requires careful consideration of the context in which they operated. The king's declining health, the ongoing threat from Saladin, and the internal conflicts within the court all created an exceptionally challenging environment for anyone attempting to advise him. The constant threat of conspiracies, assassinations and political subterfuge made advising the king a dangerous profession.

The selection process for advisors itself reveals much about the political realities of the kingdom. Baldwin IV, despite his illness, showed a remarkable political acumen in choosing individuals for key positions; however, the process was inevitably influenced by factors beyond merit alone. Family connections, personal loyalties, and the strategic need to balance competing factions all played crucial roles in the appointment of key advisors. The king's decisions reflected a deep understanding of the complex dynamics of the Crusader court. He skillfully used these appointments to balance power, creating a fragile equilibrium that often teetered on the brink of collapse.

The impact of advisors extended beyond their formal roles; they often exerted influence through informal networks and patronage systems. The distribution of patronage, the allocation of resources, and the promotion of individuals within the court were all influenced by the advisors' connections and alliances. This network of power shaped the everyday life of the court, determining who gained favor and who fell out of grace.

The interplay between these advisors and ministers was not harmonious. Their conflicting loyalties, ambitions, and strategies created a dynamic and often volatile political environment. Open confrontations were not uncommon, with alliances shifting as quickly as the sands of the desert. This constant political maneuvering shaped the king's decisions and, consequently, the destiny of the kingdom.

Baldwin IV's advisors, while theoretically there to assist him in governing the kingdom, often had their own agendas. Their advice was frequently tinged with self-interest and the desire to further their own ambitions, or the ambitions of their families. Determining the true motivation behind their actions is a significant challenge for historians; the sources are often fragmented, biased, and riddled with conflicting accounts. The primary sources, often written by individuals with their own vested interests, offer varying
perspectives, making objective analysis difficult.

The king's reliance on his advisors, however, highlights the limits of his power. His health, although a significant factor, was not the sole reason for the court's instability. The king, despite his intelligence and political skill, needed to rely on the advice and support of those around him. This reliance, however, created vulnerabilities, as the actions and motivations of his advisors significantly influenced the decisions he made.

The internal struggles within the court were often reflected in the king's policies. The conflicts and compromises that characterized the relationship between Baldwin IV and his advisors shaped the kingdom's foreign and domestic policies, impacting its military strategies, alliances, and internal stability. The constant political maneuvering created an environment of uncertainty, hindering the effective implementation of long-term policies.

The political machinations of Baldwin's reign illustrate the limitations of even the most powerful ruler, even a highly skilled and intelligent one. The king's health may have compromised his ability to fully exert his power, but the inherent instability of the court, fueled by the rivalries and ambitions of his advisors, also played a significant role in shaping the outcome of his reign. In conclusion, the story of Baldwin IV's advisors is not merely a series of individual biographies; it is a crucial element in understanding the complexities of the Crusader states, the challenges faced by its rulers, and the ultimate downfall of the kingdom itself. Their actions, both noble and ignoble, had a lasting impact on the course of history, a reminder of the enduring power of political intrigue and the limitations of even the most capable of rulers. The delicate balance of power within the Crusader kingdom rested not solely on the king's shoulders but also on the treacherous terrain navigated by his advisors and the often-conflicting interests they represented.

Chapter 14

Internal Conflicts and Conspiracies Maintaining Control

The precarious balance of power within the Kingdom of Jerusalem, even under the strong leadership of Baldwin IV, was constantly threatened by internal conflicts and conspiracies. These weren't merely isolated incidents; they were a persistent feature of court life, reflecting the inherent instability of a kingdom built on precarious alliances and competing ambitions. Baldwin, despite his considerable intelligence and strategic acumen, faced a relentless struggle to maintain control, a struggle exacerbated by his debilitating illness.

One of the most significant sources of conflict stemmed from the succession question. Baldwin IV, knowing his life was tragically short, lacked a legitimate heir. This absence created a power vacuum, fueling speculation and maneuvering amongst the powerful families of the kingdom. The potential successors, each with their own supporters and factions, openly and covertly competed for influence, undermining Baldwin's authority and destabilizing the realm. The most prominent contenders were, of course, members of the powerful Lusignan family and the relatives of other leading nobles. Each potential claimant gathered support and resources, creating rival factions that frequently clashed within the court. These internal divisions often mirrored broader political and religious factions within the kingdom, creating a complex web of alliances and rivalries.

The rivalry between the Lusignan family, particularly Guy de Lusignan, and Raymond III of Tripoli exemplifies this struggle for power. While Raymond, a seasoned veteran of the Crusader states and a man of considerable prestige, enjoyed the support of a significant portion of the kingdom's nobility, Guy's rise was a more meteoric one. His ambition and his marriage to Sibylla, Baldwin's sister and a potential heiress to the throne, propelled him into a prominent position, making him a serious contender for the crown. The conflict between these two men wasn't just a personal rivalry; it represented a wider struggle between established aristocratic families and a newer, more ambitious family attempting to assert its dominance. Their competition for influence often spilled over into an open conflict, creating instability within the kingdom and weakening Baldwin IV's position.

The fragility of Baldwin's authority was further underscored by several notable conspiracies. The exact details of these plots remain shrouded in historical ambiguity, due to the conflicting accounts and the deliberate obfuscation of participants. However, it's clear that various factions within the kingdom attempted to undermine the king, often using methods ranging from subtle political maneuvering to outright assassination attempts. These conspiracies were fueled by personal ambitions, religious differences, and the desire to shape the kingdom's future according to the conspirators' own interests. The failure of these conspiracies to succeed doesn't diminish their significance; they serve as a testament to the pervasive instability and the constant threat to the king's authority.

One such conspiracy involved the attempt to marry Sibylla to a man who would support the conspirators' aims rather than to Guy. This plot represented a direct challenge to the Lusignans, and its failure further solidified Guy's position, setting the stage for future conflicts. The details of this plot are scarce, but the fact of its existence reveals the depth of the political intrigue at the heart of Baldwin's court.

Furthermore, the religious context of the Crusader states added another layer of complexity to the internal conflicts. The Patriarch of Jerusalem, as mentioned previously, wielded immense religious and political power. His relationship with Baldwin IV was often characterized by tension, particularly when the Patriarch's actions seemed to favor certain noble families or political agendas, thus adding to the already volatile situation at court. The church's influence over the population added a further dimension to the internal power struggles, as support from religious figures could significantly bolster a political faction's strength and legitimacy.

Baldwin IV, despite his physical limitations, proved to be a shrewd and resilient ruler. He skillfully navigated the treacherous political landscape, expertly playing various factions against each other to maintain a fragile balance of power. However, this equilibrium was constantly threatened. He employed a variety of strategies to combat internal strife, including carefully selecting advisors who could counterbalance each other's influence, and utilizing patronage to reward loyalty while isolating potential enemies. He also acted decisively, when necessary, swiftly suppressing rebellions and punishing conspirators. The king understood the importance of demonstrating strength, even while battling his debilitating illness. His very survival, against incredible odds, served as a symbol of his resilience and determination, inspiring loyalty from some and fear from others.

The constant threat of internal conflict greatly impacted Baldwin's ability to govern effectively. The time and energy he expended managing internal disputes diverted resources and attention from the kingdom's external threats, primarily the growing power of Saladin. This internal instability created a situation where he needed to focus on maintaining control instead of implementing long-term strategies for the benefit of the kingdom. The constant need to balance competing factions within his court made it difficult to formulate and execute coherent policies regarding military campaigns, economic reforms or even internal administration.

The consequences of these internal conflicts were profound and far-reaching. They weakened the kingdom's defenses, created divisions within its population, and ultimately contributed to its decline. The constant struggle for power, the never-ending series of conspiracies, and the shifting alliances left the kingdom vulnerable to external threats. Saladin's ultimate victory over the Crusader states can, in part, be attributed to the chronic internal instability that had plagued the kingdom for years, sapping its strength and unity. The political maneuvering, infighting, and ambition of Baldwin's court directly contributed to the weakened state of the kingdom's defenses and its eventual fall from power.

In analyzing Baldwin IV's reign, it's crucial to avoid portraying him simply as a victim of circumstance. While his illness undoubtedly presented significant challenges, his ability to maintain control for so long, in the face of such intense internal opposition, was a testament to his political skill and unwavering determination. His reign showcases a king desperately fighting to keep his kingdom together, forced to deal with not only external enemies, but also a relentless war within his own court. The internal conflicts and conspiracies of Baldwin IV's reign are not simply a historical curiosity; they are a vital component in understanding the rise and fall of the Kingdom of Jerusalem, illustrating the fragility of power, even in the hands of a brilliant and determined leader. The relentless struggle for control within the court ultimately contributed to the kingdom's weakness and vulnerability, making it easier prey for its powerful neighbors. The story of Baldwin IV is not just a tale of a king fighting a devastating disease; it is a gripping narrative of a leader locked in a constant battle for survival against the insidious and relentless forces of internal conflict and political intrigue. The fragility of the Crusader states is clearly depicted in the tumultuous events of Baldwin's court, a microcosm of the larger political landscape of the time. The lasting impact of this internal strife underlines the crucial role of internal stability in maintaining the power and longevity of any kingdom.

Chapter 15

Managing the Barons Balancing Power and Authority

The precariousness of Baldwin IV's position stemmed not only from external threats, but also, and perhaps more significantly, from the volatile dynamics within his own kingdom. Ruling the Kingdom of Jerusalem meant navigating a complex web of powerful baronial families, each vying for influence and control. These weren't simply loyal subjects; they were ambitious individuals and families who held considerable power, often exceeding the king's direct authority within their fiefdoms. Baldwin, despite his military prowess and strategic brilliance, faced the constant challenge of managing these powerful barons, balancing their competing ambitions and preventing the disintegration of his kingdom into warring factions.

One of Baldwin's primary strategies for managing his barons was the skillful use of diplomacy and patronage. He understood the importance of cultivating loyalties through strategic alliances and carefully distributing favors. This wasn't simply about bribery; it was about creating a system of reciprocal obligations, ensuring that the barons felt invested in his success and their own well-being. He rewarded loyalty with land grants, lucrative positions in his court, and strategic marriages that solidified political bonds. By carefully distributing these rewards, Baldwin attempted to create a delicate balance of power, preventing any single family or faction from becoming too dominant.

However, diplomacy alone was insufficient. Baldwin was acutely aware that the barons' ambitions were often insatiable, and their loyalty could be fleeting. Therefore, he also employed a more assertive approach, demonstrating a willingness to use force when necessary. The suppression of rebellions, both large and small, was crucial in maintaining order and reinforcing the king's authority.

Baldwin's actions weren't merely punitive; they served as a deterrent, demonstrating that challenging his rule would have serious consequences. This strategic mix of rewarding loyalty and punishing dissent was vital in maintaining the fragile equilibrium of power within his kingdom.

The key to understanding Baldwin's approach lies in appreciating the intricate web of alliances and rivalries that characterized the Crusader states. He strategically played these factions against each other, preventing anyone from becoming too powerful. He carefully cultivated relationships with specific barons, using them as counterweights against others. This required a keen understanding of personality, ambition, and the shifting dynamics of power within the nobility. He understood the importance of maintaining a balance, ensuring that no single faction felt empowered enough to openly challenge his authority.

The challenge was further complicated by the religious dimension of the Crusader states. The Patriarch of Jerusalem held immense religious and political influence, capable of swaying public opinion and mobilizing support for factions. Baldwin's relationship with the Patriarch was often fraught with tension, as he had to navigate the complex interplay between secular and religious authority. He had to manage the Patriarch's influence while simultaneously dealing with the ambitions of the powerful baronial families. This delicate balancing act required considerable political acumen and a deep understanding of the nuances of religious and political power.

Furthermore, the ongoing conflict with the Muslim world added another layer of complexity to Baldwin's challenges. External threats often exacerbated internal tensions, as the barons could use the necessity of defense against Saladin to consolidate power or push for greater autonomy. Baldwin had to continuously balance the need for unified defense against the risk of empowering his baronial rivals through the distribution of military commands and resources. This necessitated an intricate strategy where he employed a variety of tactics to maintain both external and internal security.

The succession crisis further aggravated the situation. Baldwin IV, aware of his deteriorating health, faced the daunting task of securing his legacy and preventing a power struggle after his death. The lack of a clear heir created a vacuum that numerous ambitious nobles sought to fill. He had to find a way to manage potential successors without alienating key players or provoking open conflict. He made various attempts to secure a succession plan, but the inherent unpredictability of court politics and the ambitions of powerful families constantly threatened to derail his efforts.

The problem extended beyond simply managing individual barons. Baldwin also had to contend with the complex network of alliances and rivalries amongst them. These alliances shifted constantly, with barons forming and dissolving partnerships based on their immediate interests and perceptions of power dynamics. This fluid system required Baldwin to be perpetually vigilant and adaptable, constantly recalibrating his strategies to maintain a balance of power. One moment, a baron might be a crucial ally; the next, he could be a potential enemy.

One specific example of Baldwin's efforts involved his careful selection and deployment of advisors. He understood the importance of having a council that represented a broad range of interests while preventing any one member from becoming too influential. He appointed individuals from different families and backgrounds, ensuring a balance of perspectives. This deliberate strategy prevented the concentration of power and provided a counterbalance to the ambitions of the barons. The advisors, in turn, played a critical role in mediating disputes and advising the king on how best to handle the ever-shifting political landscape.

Managing his barons, therefore, was not a singular task, but a continuous process demanding relentless vigilance, strategic maneuvering, and a willingness to use both diplomacy and force.

Baldwin IV's success in maintaining a semblance of order for as long as he did was a testament to his exceptional political skills, despite the profound limitations imposed by his illness. His approach highlights the intricate challenges faced by rulers in medieval societies, where maintaining a balance of power was crucial for survival. The complexities of his reign underscore the fact that the decline of the Crusader Kingdom was not solely a result of external pressures, but also, significantly, a consequence of internal instability and the king's constant struggle to control the ambitions of his powerful vassals. The story of Baldwin IV is a powerful reminder of the fragility of power and the constant balancing act required to maintain order in a world defined by competing ambitions.

Chapter 16

The Progression of Leprosy and its Physical Impact Limitations and Adaptations

The relentless progression of Baldwin IV's leprosy cast a long shadow over his reign, gradually eroding his physical capabilities and presenting ever-increasing challenges to his governance. While the early stages of the disease may have been relatively manageable, allowing him to pursue rigorous military training and even display remarkable prowess on the battlefield, its insidious advance dramatically altered the course of his life and the stability of the Kingdom of Jerusalem. The physical manifestations of the disease, initially subtle, became increasingly debilitating, affecting not only his appearance but also his ability to perform the essential functions of kingship.

The most visible symptom was, of course, the disfiguring lesions that marred his skin. These lesions, initially localized, spread gradually across his body, causing significant disfigurement. While accounts vary in detail, contemporary chronicles and later artistic representations paint a picture of progressive deterioration, with lesions affecting his face, hands, and limbs. The descriptions suggest not only the aesthetic impact but also the constant pain and discomfort these lesions would have caused, hindering everyday activities and significantly affecting his physical presence in court and on the battlefield. The gradual loss of facial features likely impacted his ability to project the authority and charisma expected of a king. The physical pain alone must have been immense, a constant reminder of the disease's relentless grip.

Beyond the visible lesions, leprosy attacked the nervous system, causing numbness, paralysis, and a gradual loss of sensation. This had profound implications for Baldwin's military capabilities. His skill in horsemanship, once a source of pride and a key component of his authority, must have been progressively compromised by the disease. The subtle loss of dexterity in his hands, the gradual weakening of his limbs, and the increasing numbness would have hampered his ability to wield a sword effectively or to control a horse with the precision required for battle. His legendary battlefield victories were undoubtedly achieved with increasing difficulty as his disease progressed. The chronicles, while celebrating his military successes, do not fully convey the physical strain and pain he endured during these campaigns.

The impact on his daily life was equally significant. Simple tasks, such as writing, eating, and dressing, would have become increasingly arduous and potentially painful. The loss of sensation could have led to accidental injuries, further complicating his health. Even the act of attending court, a crucial aspect of his kingship, must have become a physical ordeal. He was forced to rely more heavily on advisors and intermediaries to fulfill the duties expected of him, leading to a potential erosion of his direct control and increasing reliance on others. This shift in the dynamic power within the court undoubtedly created new vulnerabilities and opportunities for intrigue among his ambitious barons.

The physical limitations imposed by leprosy also affected Baldwin's ability to maintain personal relationships. While accounts of his personal life are scant, the disfigurement associated with the disease would inevitably have impacted his personal interactions. The social stigma surrounding leprosy in medieval society would have further isolated him, limiting the closeness and intimacy of his relationships. The king, so admired and revered on the battlefield, was likely forced to confront a deep sense of isolation and personal vulnerability as his physical appearance changed. This personal struggle must have added another layer of complexity to his already immense political burdens.

However, Baldwin IV's story is not one of mere decline and suffering. It is also a testament to his remarkable resilience and adaptation. Facing the relentless progression of his disease, he devised innovative strategies to compensate for his physical limitations and maintain his authority. While his military prowess was undeniably compromised, he compensated by honing his strategic abilities. His battlefield decisions, increasingly reliant on accurate assessments and astute tactical planning, demonstrated a strategic genius that compensated for his diminishing physical capabilities. His victories were no longer solely a matter of personal strength and courage, but also of carefully calculated maneuvers and alliances.

Furthermore, he adapted his governance to accommodate his physical limitations. He relied more heavily on his advisors, delegating responsibilities and cultivating a network of loyal and capable officials. This adaptation, while sometimes leading to internal conflicts, also allowed him to maintain a semblance of control amidst the challenges posed by ambitious barons and external threats. The council he assembled, though at times fractured by internal disputes, was crucial in managing the affairs of the kingdom during the king's progressively worsening health. This shift towards a more collaborative form of governance, while necessitated by his illness, might even have strengthened certain aspects of his reign.

Baldwin's understanding of his physical limitations also influenced his political strategies. He was acutely aware of his vulnerability and strategically used this knowledge to his advantage. He cultivated loyalties amongst his barons not solely through coercion or reward, but also by fostering a sense of shared responsibility and shared peril. His clear-sighted acknowledgment of his condition might have engendered a deeper sense of loyalty amongst those who served him, recognizing their essential role in maintaining the stability of the kingdom in the face of his physical decline. This understanding of his own limitations fostered a dynamic of
collaboration within the court.

His efforts to secure the succession also reflect his pragmatic adaptation to his illness. Despite the constant threat of internal conflict and the ambitions of those vying for power, he made multiple attempts to ensure a stable transfer of authority, reflecting his understanding of the precarious nature of his position and the need to prepare for his eventual incapacity. These attempts, although ultimately unsuccessful, demonstrate a profound commitment to the welfare of his kingdom, even in the face of his own inevitable death. The complexity of the succession crisis, therefore, was not solely a product of the political machines of the barons, but also a reflection of Baldwin's illness and its profound impact on the stability of the kingdom.

The worsening of Baldwin IV's leprosy was not merely a personal tragedy; it was a crucial catalyst in the unraveling of the Kingdom of Jerusalem. The disease profoundly affected his physical and mental capacity, directly impacting his ability to perform the essential functions of kingship. While his resilience and strategic brilliance allowed him to compensate for some of these limitations, the constant physical pain, the increasing reliance on others, and the progressive erosion of his authority created a vacuum that opportunistic nobles eagerly sought to fill. The story of Baldwin IV, therefore, serves as a powerful reminder that the fate of even the most capable rulers can be tragically shaped by the relentless forces of nature. His struggle with leprosy highlights the intimate link between personal health, political power, and the overall stability of the medieval Crusader states. The king's decline mirrors the kingdom's own fragility, and the inherent instability present in a land always teetering on the edge of war and internal conflict. His story serves as a compelling case study demonstrating the complex intersection between personal health, political strategy, and the fate of a kingdom. The relentless advance of leprosy was not only a personal affliction, but also a crucial factor in the tragic decline of the Kingdom of Jerusalem.

Chapter 17

The Struggle for Succession Sibylla and the Claimants to the Throne

The final years of Baldwin IV's reign were consumed by a desperate struggle for succession, a struggle as debilitating to the Kingdom of Jerusalem as the king's own affliction. The looming question of who would inherit the throne became a battleground for ambitious nobles, each maneuvering for advantage amidst the growing uncertainty. The king's deteriorating health, the visible manifestation of his leprosy, fueled the escalating tensions within the court, transforming the already fragile political landscape into a maelstrom of competing claims and shifting alliances.

The most prominent contender for the throne was Sibylla, Baldwin's sister. Her marriage to William of Montferrat, a powerful and ambitious nobleman, solidified her position as a significant player in the succession crisis. Sibylla, however, was not without her detractors. Her perceived lack of political acumen and her husband's ambitious nature raised concern among many barons.

While her claim to the throne was undeniable through her royal bloodline, the potential for her husband to wield real power behind the scenes cast a shadow over her suitability as a ruler. The perception of William as a potential puppet master, pulling the strings of a relatively inexperienced queen, caused distrust amongst a substantial segment of the court, who feared his foreign influence and perceived ambition. This deep-seated concern would have significant ramifications for the stability of the kingdom and fueled much of the opposition to Sibylla's claim.

Adding complexity to the situation was the presence of Baldwin's nephew, Baldwin of Montferrat (son of Sibylla's brother, Amalric I), a young boy who, despite his tender age, represented a potential alternative. The support for young Baldwin stemmed from the hope that a regency could be established during his minority, preventing the immediate and potentially destabilizing rule of William of Montferrat.

This faction, comprising many of the kingdom's more conservative elements, viewed young Baldwin as a symbol of stability, believing a regency council could better manage the kingdom's affairs than a ruler potentially influenced by foreign ambitions. The inherent problem with this solution was the precariousness of a regency, historically prone to factional infighting and power struggles. The very council meant to ensure stability could easily become the source of further division and strife.

The situation was further complicated by the ambitions of other powerful figures within the kingdom, each with their own agendas and alliances. Raymond III of Tripoli, one of the kingdom's most powerful and experienced barons, represented a significant force, carefully maneuvering to secure his position and influence regardless of the ultimate outcome. His longstanding experience in the political machinations of the Crusader states placed him in a unique position to shape events, adding to the already volatile mix of competing ambitions and strategic maneuvering. Raymond, possessing considerable influence and military might, held the potential to either solidify the reign of a chosen successor or trigger further conflict. His strategic decisions in the following years would prove pivotal in determining the trajectory of the Kingdom of Jerusalem.

Adding another layer to the complexity of the succession crisis was the ever-present threat of external enemies. The Muslim states surrounding the Kingdom of Jerusalem, always poised to capitalize on internal strife, presented a constant and dangerous pressure on the fractious court. The stability of the kingdom was directly dependent upon a strong and unified leadership capable of repelling these external threats. The ongoing struggle for succession created a perfect opportunity for the kingdom's enemies to exploit its vulnerabilities. The very real fear of external invasion served to heighten the urgency of the succession crisis, pressuring nobles to make choices not only based on personal ambition but also on the imperative of maintaining the kingdom's survival.

Baldwin IV, despite his worsening condition, remained acutely aware of the dangers of a disputed succession. He attempted to manipulate events to his advantage, employing a series of strategic maneuvers designed to ensure a relatively stable transition of power. He made several attempts to secure a marriage alliance for Sibylla that would either neutralize William's influence or provide an alternative heir to the throne. These intricate negotiations reflect a deep understanding of the political chess game he was playing. His attempts to control the succession, however, were hampered by the ambitions of his barons and the inherent instability of the court. The king's influence was waning, despite his attempts to remain in control.

The king's attempts to secure a stable succession were frequently undermined by the political realities of the situation. The ambitions of the various claimants, the shifting alliances, and the deep-seated rivalries among the barons created an environment of almost constant intrigue. The political maneuvering became increasingly sophisticated, with secret alliances and betrayals becoming commonplace. This intense political rivalry had a corrosive impact on the kingdom, diverting resources and attention away from the urgent challenges of defending the kingdom against external threats. The internal conflicts served to weaken the kingdom significantly, leaving it exposed and vulnerable.

The king's attempts to control the narrative of his succession were constantly frustrated by the various factions at court. Even as Baldwin IV struggled to implement his carefully considered plans, he was continually countered by the machinations of his nobles. This struggle highlights the limitations of even the most astute ruler facing an environment of deep-seated political division and the conflicting ambitions of his barons. The inability of the king to enforce his will underscores the deep-seated flaws in the political system, flaws which were ultimately responsible for the eventual fall of the Kingdom.

In the end, Baldwin IV's efforts to secure a stable succession proved largely unsuccessful. His health continued to deteriorate, leaving him increasingly reliant on others, who often acted more for their own interests than for the good of the kingdom. The period leading up to his death was one of escalating tension and political maneuvering. The struggle for the throne was not only a struggle for power but also a struggle for the very survival of the Kingdom of Jerusalem. The eventual consequences of this power struggle would have dramatic and lasting repercussions for the kingdom, setting in motion a series of events that would ultimately lead to its decline and fragmentation.

The succession crisis was not simply a contest between individual ambitions, but also a reflection of the deeper structural weaknesses within the Crusader kingdom. The feudal system, with its inherent tensions between the king and his barons, was ill-equipped to handle a situation as volatile as the crisis triggered by Baldwin IV's illness. The fragmented nature of the kingdom, with its various fiefdoms and powerful lords, meant that any single ruler would face tremendous challenges in asserting control. The absence of strong centralized authority further exacerbated the problem.

The events surrounding Baldwin IV's death and the subsequent struggle for succession reveal the complex interplay of factors that contributed to the decline of the Kingdom of Jerusalem. It was not merely a case of individual failings but a convergence of political, social, and religious forces that ultimately led to the kingdom's undoing. The escalating succession crisis highlighted the fundamental instability at the heart of the Crusader states, an instability that would continue to haunt the kingdom in the years to come. The seeds of the kingdom's ultimate demise were sown in these final, desperate years of Baldwin IV's reign, a testament to the vulnerability of even the most powerful kingdoms when faced with internal division and the relentless pressures of political ambition. The legacy of Baldwin IV's reign is a profound and complicated one, marked by both extraordinary military triumphs and heartbreaking political failures, ultimately emphasizing the fragility of power in the medieval world and the persistent dangers of unchecked ambition.

Chapter 18

Negotiations and Compromises Attempts to Secure a Stable Succession

The desperate scramble for succession following Baldwin IV's failing health wasn't merely a clash of egos; it was a complex tapestry woven from threads of familial ties, political maneuvering, and the ever-present threat of external enemies. Baldwin IV, acutely aware of the kingdom's vulnerability, initiated a series of negotiations and compromises aimed at preventing a catastrophic civil war. His primary concern was to avoid the chaos that would inevitably benefit the kingdom's Muslim neighbors. The king, despite his physical decline, remained a shrewd political player, utilizing his waning influence to attempt to shape the future of Jerusalem.

His first significant attempt centered around his sister Sibylla and her husband, William of Montferrat. William, a powerful and ambitious nobleman, posed a considerable threat. His potential to dominate the court in the event of Sibylla's ascension raised alarm bells amongst many barons, who feared the implications of a foreign-born regent potentially dictating the Kingdom's policies. To mitigate this risk, Baldwin attempted to negotiate a compromise that would limit William's influence while still securing Sibylla's claim to the throne. He explored various options, including seeking a new marriage for Sibylla, a union that might produce a more acceptable heir and potentially neutralize William's ambition.

Several prominent noblemen were considered, but the political intricacies proved insurmountable. Each potential suitor held their own power base and allegiance, and negotiating a marriage acceptable to all parties proved to be a herculean task. The barons, deeply divided amongst themselves and wary of any perceived usurpation of their power, proved resistant to compromise.

The discussions regarding Sibylla's future were often fraught with tension. The barons' objections weren't solely directed towards William; they also stemmed from lingering doubts about Sibylla's abilities as a ruler. Many believed her to be lacking the necessary political acumen to effectively govern the volatile kingdom. Their concerns were not unfounded, given the history of female rulers in the Crusader states, who often faced greater challenges in maintaining authority and stability compared to their male counterparts. This prejudice, ingrained in the feudal society of the time, further complicated the already delicate negotiations. The king's attempts to negotiate a solution acceptable to all factions foundered on the rocks of personal ambition and deep-seated mistrust.

Simultaneously, Baldwin IV explored the possibility of establishing a regency council to govern the kingdom during the minority of his young nephew, Baldwin of Montferrat. This plan, while seemingly straightforward, presented its own set of challenges. Determining the composition of this council and establishing a clear hierarchy of authority proved exceptionally difficult. Each baron sought to secure a place within the regency, aiming to maximize their influence over the young king and the administration of the kingdom. The very individuals meant to ensure stability were often the ones actively undermining it, as their own self-interest took precedence over the collective good. The discussions were marked by intense lobbying, veiled threats, and blatant displays of power, mirroring the larger struggle for succession that was raging beyond the confines of the negotiating chambers.

Raymond III of Tripoli, one of the most powerful and experienced barons, played a critical role in these negotiations. His strategic acumen and deep understanding of the kingdom's political landscape allowed him to maneuver skillfully, weighing the strengths and weaknesses of each proposal. He wasn't merely an observer; he actively participated, offering counsel, leveraging his influence, and ultimately shaping the direction of the discussions.

His neutrality, however, was not absolute. Raymond's own ambitions remained a significant factor in his decisions, adding yet another layer of complexity to the already turbulent political scene. He carefully cultivated his relationships with the various factions, ensuring that he retained a degree of influence irrespective of who eventually ascended the throne.

The negotiations were not confined to the court; they extended to the realm's religious leaders. The Patriarch of Jerusalem and other ecclesiastical dignitaries possessed considerable influence over the barons and the populace. Their support, or lack thereof, could significantly impact the success or failure of any proposed succession plan. Securing their endorsement required a delicate balancing act, as their own agendas, which often intertwined with matters of religious doctrine and political power, added to the intricacy of the process. This needs to secure the church's support added another dimension to the king's already challenging task.

The ever-present external threat further complicated the delicate balance of power. The Muslim rulers of Egypt and Syria watched the unfolding drama with keen interest, waiting for the opportune moment to exploit any weakness within the Kingdom. The constant threat of invasion served as a stark reminder of the urgent need for stable and unified leadership. The ongoing negotiations were therefore conducted against a backdrop of escalating external pressure, underscoring the critical importance of resolving the succession crisis before the kingdom imploded under its own internal divisions.

Despite Baldwin IV's tireless efforts, a complete resolution proved elusive. His attempts to secure a stable succession were consistently hampered by the deeply entrenched rivalries and the overwhelming ambition of the kingdom's most influential nobles. The king's influence, already diminished by his illness, was further eroded by his inability to fully control the machinations of his court. Each compromise reached was fragile, constantly threatened by shifting alliances and unexpected betrayals. The fragile peace built through negotiation frequently fractured under the weight of personal ambitions and political maneuvering.

The compromises and negotiations were never truly successful in achieving a lasting peace. They represented a desperate, albeit largely unsuccessful, attempt to stave off an inevitable conflict. The underlying tension remained, constantly bubbling beneath the surface, threatening to erupt at any moment. The period leading up to Baldwin IV's death was characterized by a series of increasingly fragile truces, each more tenuous than the last. The final years of his reign were a masterclass in political maneuvering, yet ultimately a testament to the limitations of power in the face of deep-seated internal divisions. The failure to secure a stable succession wasn't simply a matter of miscalculation or bad luck; it was a reflection of the inherent flaws within the Crusader Kingdom's political system, flaws that would ultimately contribute to its demise. The relentless pressures of ambition, coupled with the external threats, proved insurmountable, leaving the kingdom teetering on the precipice of collapse. The legacy of Baldwin IV's attempts at peaceful succession serves as a sobering reminder of the fragility of even the most powerful realms when confronted with internecine conflict.

Chapter 19

Baldwins Final Decisions Shaping the Future of the Kingdom

The final months of Baldwin IV's life were a desperate race against time, a frantic attempt to secure a future for the Kingdom of Jerusalem that would not succumb to the chaos threatening to engulf it. His deteriorating health, ravaged by leprosy, mirrored the crumbling stability of his realm. The king, despite his physical frailty, maintained a sharp mind and an unwavering commitment to his kingdom's survival. His choices, however, were severely
constrained by the limitations imposed by his illness and the deep-seated ambitions of the powerful barons who surrounded him.

His initial attempts to manage the succession centered around his sister, Sibylla. The marriage to William of Montferrat remained a significant hurdle. While William possessed military prowess and political acumen, his foreign origins and his ambitious nature created a deep unease amongst the kingdom's barons. They feared the potential for a foreign-dominated court, one that might
prioritize the interests of William's family and supporters of the kingdom's welfare. The barons' concerns were not unfounded; the history of the Crusader states was filled with examples of ambitious nobles leveraging their position to undermine the authority of the reigning monarch.

Baldwin IV attempted several strategies to reconcile the barons'anxieties with Sibylla's claim. He considered arranging a new marriage for his sister, a union that could potentially produce a more acceptable heir and alleviate concerns about William's undue influence. The problem, however, lay in the scarcity of suitable candidates. Any nobleman of sufficient power to solidify Sibylla's position also held significant ambitions of their own. The king's attempts to negotiate a politically advantageous marriage – one that wouldn't upset the delicate balance of power – repeatedly foundered. The constant maneuvering, the shifting alliances, and the blatant self-interest of the various barons proved too significant an obstacle.

Furthermore, doubts regarding Sibylla's ability to rule independently added complexity to the succession question. Many barons viewed her as lacking the necessary political skills to govern the kingdom effectively. The prevailing prejudice against female rulers in the medieval world played a crucial role in undermining her authority and generating opposition to her claim. While Sibylla might have been capable, the prevailing social norms presented a significant obstacle to her acceptance as the sole ruler. Baldwin IV's attempts to navigate this deeply entrenched prejudice within the kingdom's power structure added another layer to the existing complexities of the succession crisis.

The alternative Baldwin IV explored was establishing a regency council to govern the kingdom during the minority of his young nephew, Baldwin of Montferrat. This young boy, a relative through marriage, represented a less contentious alternative to Sibylla.

However, the formation of a stable regency council proved as challenging as resolving Sibylla's succession. The process of selecting members, defining their roles and powers, and establishing a clear chain of command exposed the same fractures and ambitions within the noble class. Each baron lobbied fiercely, maneuvering to secure a position that would maximize their power and influence over the young king and the kingdom's administration. The very mechanism intended to secure stability risked becoming a source of further instability and conflict.

Raymond III of Tripoli, a seasoned and politically astute baron, played a pivotal role in these negotiations. His wisdom and experience allowed him to see the weaknesses of every proposal, to understand the motivations of the various players, and to attempt to guide the process towards a compromise. He was adept at navigating the tangled web of personal rivalries and ambitions.

However, even Raymond's influence wasn't absolute. His own aspirations undoubtedly impacted on his choices, adding another layer of complexity to an already precarious situation. His carefully crafted neutrality allowed him to maintain influence regardless of who eventually secured the throne, a testament to his political savvy.

The Church also played a significant part in these critical decisions. The Patriarch of Jerusalem and other influential religious figures wielded considerable authority and influence. Securing their approval for any succession plan was essential for its success. However, their involvement introduced another dimension to the negotiations, as the Church's interests and priorities, often interwoven with religious doctrines and political power, complicated the already complex scenario. The king had to balance the concerns of the secular and religious powers, a task that increased the difficulty of finding a lasting solution.

The external threats from Muslim rulers in Egypt and Syria added urgency to the unfolding drama. They keenly observed the kingdom's internal struggles, awaiting the opportune moment to exploit any weakness and potentially launch an invasion. The ever-present threat of war heightened the need for unified and stable leadership. This precarious situation compelled Baldwin IV to act quickly, but his efforts were consistently hampered by the relentless ambitions and rivalries of the barons.

Baldwin IV's final decisions reflected his desperate attempts to prevent the kingdom's collapse. His efforts to secure a peaceful succession, however, were consistently undermined by the kingdom's deep-seated divisions. His weakened condition, caused by the relentless advance of leprosy, eroded his ability to completely control the court's machines. Each seemingly successful compromise proved to be fragile, constantly threatened by shifting alliances and sudden betrayals. The short-lived periods of tranquility was quickly shattered by the relentless pursuit of personal power. The intense pressures of internal ambition, combined with external threats, proved overwhelming. Baldwin IV's legacy in these final years demonstrates the limitations of even the most skilled ruler's power when faced with relentless internal conflict.

His failure to secure a stable succession was not merely a result of poor judgment or miscalculation. It reflected deeper issues inherent within the political structure of the Crusader Kingdom – a system plagued by unchecked ambition and inherent instability. This ultimately contributed to the kingdom's eventual decline. The struggle for the throne wasn't simply a matter of chance or misfortune, but a consequence of the deep flaws within the system. The story of Baldwin IV's final decisions serves as a poignant reminder of the fragility of even the most powerful kingdoms when confronted with intractable internal divisions. His attempts to safeguard his realm's future, despite the constraints of his illness and the unrestrained ambitions of his nobles, offer a stark lesson in the complexities of medieval power politics. The ensuing chaos and conflict that followed his death were, in many ways, a direct consequence of the choices made – or rather, the compromises that proved ultimately impossible to sustain – during these crucial final months. The legacy of Baldwin IV's efforts remains a powerful testament to the enduring challenges of maintaining order and stability in a world characterized by relentless ambition and the constant threat of external aggression.

Chapter 20

The Last Days of King Baldwin IV A Legacy of Strength and Resilience

The relentless progression of leprosy relentlessly eroded Baldwin IV's physical strength, yet his mental acuity remained surprisingly sharp. Even as his body succumbed to the disease, his mind continued to grapple with the intricate political landscape of the Kingdom of Jerusalem, a kingdom increasingly fractured by ambition and internal strife. His final days were marked not by despair, but by a grim determination to secure a stable future for his realm, a future increasingly threatened by the very people he had entrusted with its governance.

Reports from the court paint a picture of a king struggling to maintain his authority. The physical toll of the leprosy was evident– the visible disfigurement, the constant pain, the progressive loss of physical function. Yet, accounts suggest that even in his weakened state, he remained deeply involved in state affairs, dictating decrees, reviewing petitions, and holding audiences with his advisors, often from his bedchamber. The sheer effort required for these activities speaks volumes about his dedication to his duty, his unwavering commitment to the kingdom he had defended so fiercely. Chronicles of the time detail his continued interest in military matters, meticulously reviewing troop deployments and strategy, demonstrating a remarkable continued engagement in a role his physical condition increasingly limited. He might have been confined to his bed or a litter, but his influence within the court, his mental grip on power, remained formidable.

His relationship with Raymond III of Tripoli deepened during these final months. Raymond, a seasoned and pragmatic leader, served as a vital confidante and advisor. He offered crucial counsel on succession, navigating the treacherous currents of court politics with remarkable dexterity. While Raymond's loyalty to the crown was undeniable, his own political ambitions were ever-present, a delicate balance that Baldwin IV carefully managed. They were engaged in a complex, almost unspoken negotiation, a dance of trust and strategic maneuvering, where each move had to consider the other's motivations, the ever-present threats from within and

without the kingdom. Trust between them, built over years of shared challenges, was a vital asset in these turbulent times. The extent to which their conversations focused on strategies to counter external threats versus internal machinations remains a subject of scholarly debate, underscoring the difficulties inherent in

interpreting the motives of medieval rulers and their advisors.

The succession remained the central preoccupation of Baldwin's final days. His attempts to secure a stable transition of power were thwarted not simply by the ambitions of individual nobles, but by a deeply entrenched system that fostered such ambition. The feudal structure of the kingdom, with its system of fiefs and loyalties, allowed powerful barons to wield considerable influence, often at the expense of the crown. Baldwin had repeatedly attempted to balance the competing interests of these barons, often resorting to complex compromises to maintain a fragile equilibrium. However, the underlying tensions, fueled by personal rivalries and greed, proved impossible to completely suppress.

The situation with Sibylla and William of Montferrat remained unresolved. Despite the king's efforts, the opposition to William persisted. Concerns about his foreign origins and potentially destabilizing ambitions proved too difficult to overcome. The barons' resistance wasn't simply xenophobia; it was rooted in fear of losing their own hard-won power and influence within the kingdom. Each compromise reached concerning William's role seemed to generate new anxieties, often leading to further instability. The complex web of alliances, shifting loyalties, and secret pacts further complicated efforts to resolve the succession effectively. The lack of a clear and universally accepted successor created a power vacuum, which fueled even more ambitious maneuvering amongst the kingdom's elite.

The health of Baldwin IV deteriorated at an alarming rate in the final weeks. The leprosy advanced relentlessly, causing excruciating pain and increasing debility. Accounts suggest he was practically bedridden, reliant on his attendants for the most basic needs. Yet, the reports consistently portray him as maintaining a keen intellect and an unyielding spirit. He continued to participate in council meetings, albeit through intermediaries, remaining deeply involved in decision-making. This speaks to his dedication but also suggests the desperate measures he felt compelled to take in a situation where his inability to be physically present threatened the kingdom's stability.

His religious faith, a significant aspect of his life, remained steadfast. He sought solace and guidance from the Church, relying on prayer and religious observance to cope with both his physical suffering and the immense political burdens. The Patriarch of Jerusalem, along with other influential clergymen, played a key role in his final days, offering spiritual comfort and, undoubtedly, offering advice on matters of state. The line between religious guidance and political maneuvering in the medieval context is often blurred, a factor that needs to be considered when interpreting the actions of both Baldwin and the Church leaders.

The final days of King Baldwin IV were marked by quiet dignity, a poignant contrast to the turbulent events that surrounded him. Accounts suggest he passed away peacefully, surrounded by close advisors and religious figures. The exact date and circumstances of his death remain debated among historians, but all agree that the end came because of his unrelenting illness. While the precise accounts differ, the overall image is one of a ruler who, despite unimaginable physical suffering, maintained his composure and a strong commitment to the well-being of his kingdom until his final breath.

His death plunged the Kingdom of Jerusalem into a period of profound uncertainty. The carefully constructed compromises regarding the succession instantly fractured, replaced by open power struggles between rival factions. The absence of a strong leader amplified the pre-existing tensions, triggering a cascade of events that ultimately undermined the stability of the kingdom.

Baldwin IV's legacy extends beyond his military achievements. His perseverance in the face of severe adversity, his unwavering commitment to his kingdom despite his debilitating illness, and his strategic brilliance, even in his final days, serve as a testament to his character. He was a king who faced impossible odds, a ruler forced to grapple with internal division and external threats. While

~~his~~His efforts to prevent the kingdom's decline were ultimately unsuccessful, his story serves as a powerful reminder of the complexities of medieval power politics, the challenges of leadership in times of crisis, and the enduring human spirit's capacity to withstand the relentless tide of adversity. His story, filled with both triumph and tragedy, remains a vital and compelling narrative within the history of the Crusader states. The impact of his decisions, his struggles, and his ultimately unsuccessful efforts to ensure a peaceful succession reverberated through the subsequent history of the kingdom, ultimately contributing to its eventual demise. His life stands as a poignant example of leadership tested to its limits, illustrating the fragility of power and the enduring human struggle for stability in a constantly shifting and treacherous world.

Chapter 21

Baldwins Image in Contemporary Sources Perceptions of His Reign

Contemporary accounts of Baldwin IV's reign offer a multifaceted portrait, far removed from the romanticized image often presented in later historical narratives. While hagiographic elements occasionally appear, particularly in chronicles emphasizing his piety and fortitude, a careful analysis reveals a more nuanced and often critical perspective on his rule, reflecting the turbulent political landscape of the Kingdom of Jerusalem. These sources, ranging from official chronicles and letters to less formal accounts embedded within broader historical works, provide invaluable insight into how contemporaries perceived both the king and his impact on the kingdom.

The chroniclers of the era, often associated with specific factions within the kingdom, frequently reveal their biases in their portrayals of Baldwin IV. For instance, accounts originating from the court might emphasize the king's wisdom and unwavering commitment to justice, even in the face of his debilitating illness.

These accounts often highlight his military successes, portraying him as a skilled strategist and a courageous leader who inspired loyalty and respect among his troops. The siege of Ascalon, for example, is frequently lauded as a testament to his military prowess and his ability to unite disparate factions under a common banner, at least temporarily. However, even these ostensibly positive accounts frequently mention the challenges posed by his leprosy, subtly hinting at the limitations it imposed on his reign and the anxieties it generated within the court. The constant need for regents and advisors, even during periods of relative health, is often presented as a necessary, albeit regrettable, consequence of his illness.

Conversely, chronicles from outside the immediate court circle, particularly those written by chroniclers with connections to

pg. 117

powerful noble families, sometimes present a more critical view of Baldwin's reign. These sources frequently highlight the internal conflicts and political instability that plagued the kingdom during his rule. They often emphasize the king's struggles to maintain control over ambitious barons, whose loyalty was often conditional and their ambitions frequently at odds with the stability of the realm. The chroniclers' accounts may stress the difficulties Baldwin faced in managing the competing interests of powerful figures like Raymond III of Tripoli, or the challenges posed by the succession crisis, subtly suggesting that his illness exacerbated pre-existing political tensions rather than creating them. The increasing influence of powerful figures like Aymar of Montferrat, and the perceived weakness of Baldwin's decisions in the latter part of his reign, are occasionally portrayed as critical failures of leadership.

The chroniclers' observations reveal a keen awareness of the complex power dynamics within the kingdom, suggesting that the chroniclers themselves were involved in, or at least profoundly aware of, the intrigues surrounding the court.

The letters of the period, both personal and official, offer further insights into contemporary perceptions of Baldwin IV. Diplomatic correspondence, particularly exchanges between the king and other rulers, reveals his reputation as a formidable negotiator and a shrewd political actor. However, these letters also frequently mention the anxieties surrounding his health and the uncertainties surrounding the succession. The constant need to reassure allies and to secure military support amidst the internal conflicts underscores the precarity of the kingdom's position during his reign. Private correspondence, although less readily available, reveals more intimate aspects of the perception of Baldwin IV, offering glimpses of the king's personality and his relationships with individuals within the court. These letters are less easily accessed and often require significant historical detective work and careful textual analysis to be fully understood in context. The sheer volume of surviving correspondence, however, does suggest an active court and a considerable amount of political maneuvering.

The accounts of foreign observers, particularly those from neighboring Muslim states, offer a unique perspective on Baldwin IV's reign. These sources, often less detailed than the Christian chronicles, nevertheless provide valuable insights into the perception of Baldwin IV's military capabilities and his political influence in the region. Muslim chroniclers sometimes describe him with grudging respect, acknowledging his military talents and his ability to effectively defend his kingdom against formidable adversaries. However, their accounts tend to emphasize the internal divisions within the kingdom, portraying it as weakened by internal strife, a perception that likely contributed to Muslim ambitions for regional expansion. The differing perspectives of Christian and Muslim writers offer a compelling contrast, allowing a more comprehensive understanding of how contemporaries viewed Baldwin IV and the Kingdom of Jerusalem.

Analyzing contemporary sources requires careful consideration of their biases and limitations. The narratives are not objective accounts; rather, they reflect the perspectives and interests of their authors and the circumstances under which they were produced. Therefore, comparing multiple sources from various perspectives is crucial for reconstructing a more complete and balanced understanding of Baldwin IV's reign. Understanding the political affiliations and personal biases of the chroniclers, along with the broader context of the events, allows historians to carefully weigh the evidence and arrive at more accurate conclusions. The challenge is to synthesize the fragmented and sometimes conflicting accounts to arrive at a comprehensive image of how contemporaries saw Baldwin IV, his legacy, and his impact on the Kingdom of Jerusalem.

Even seemingly minor details within these primary sources provide valuable clues about the way contemporaries viewed Baldwin IV. The descriptions of his physical appearance, for instance, are not merely clinical observations. They often serve as metaphors for his strength of character and his ability to overcome adversity. The frequent references to his unwavering piety and his devotion to religious observance highlight the significant role religion played in shaping his image and his authority. Similarly, the accounts of his interactions with advisors and other courtiers provide a glimpse into his leadership style and his relationships with key figures within the kingdom. The frequency of accounts focusing on his interactions with Raymond III of Tripoli, for example, underlines the significance of this critical relationship in the later years of his reign.

Furthermore, analyzing the language used in these sources is vital for understanding their underlying message. The choice of words, the tone, and the emphasis on particular events all reflect the authors' biases and intentions. Identifying subtle shifts in tone or emphasis across different sources can provide critical insights into the evolving perception of Baldwin IV throughout his reign. For example, a comparison of how his military triumphs are described in early versus later chronicles can reveal shifts in the overall assessment of his leadership.

In conclusion, a thorough analysis of contemporary sources provides a compelling and nuanced understanding of how Baldwin IV was viewed by his contemporaries. Their accounts, despite their biases and limitations, offer a rich tapestry of perceptions, ranging from admiration and respect for his military skills and resilience to concerns about his ability to effectively manage the political complexities of his kingdom. The picture that emerges is not a simple narrative of a heroic king, but a far more complex portrait of a ruler striving to maintain order and stability in a tumultuous era, constantly facing challenges posed by his own illness and the relentless machinations of his court. By meticulously examining these sources, we can gain a deeper understanding of not only Baldwin IV's reign but also the political culture and power dynamics of the Kingdom of Jerusalem in the twelfth century. This contextualization allows for a far richer and more historically grounded understanding of the king's reign than any simplistic, retrospective portrayal could offer.

Chapter 22

Later Representations Legends Myths and Cultural Interpretations

The transition from contemporary accounts to later representations of Baldwin IV reveals a fascinating evolution in his image. While the twelfth-century chronicles offered a complex, often contradictory, portrait of the king, influenced by the political biases and personal perspectives of their authors, subsequent centuries witnessed a gradual shift towards a more romanticized and heroic portrayal. This transformation wasn't a singular event but a gradual process, shaped by evolving historical interpretations, the rise of nationalistic sentiments, and the changing aesthetic preferences of different eras.

The later medieval period saw Baldwin IV's story incorporated into various chronicles and histories, often with a heightened emphasis on his piety and military prowess. The focus shifted somewhat from the intricate political maneuvering and internal conflicts of his reign to a narrative centered on his personal struggle against adversity – his leprosy, and the challenges of ruling a kingdom constantly threatened by external enemies. This re-framing reflected a broader medieval interest in exemplars of faith and fortitude, where the king's resilience in the face of his illness became a powerful symbol of divine favor and unwavering devotion. His military successes, such as the victory at Montgisard, were amplified and presented as miraculous interventions, emphasizing his role as a divinely appointed defender of Christendom. These narratives, while still drawing upon earlier sources, often selectively emphasized aspects that reinforced this idealized image, minimizing or ignoring details that conflicted with this revised perspective. For example, the internal power struggles and disagreements within his court, prominently featured in contemporary accounts, were downplayed or reframed as necessary trials he overcame through his unwavering faith and exceptional leadership.

The Renaissance and early modern periods witnessed a further evolution in Baldwin's image. While still revered as a military leader, his image became increasingly intertwined with broader historical narratives of the Crusades. The narrative of the Crusades

It shifted over time, impacting how Baldwin IV's story was interpreted. In the context of burgeoning European nationalisms, Baldwin, as a Crusader king, could be claimed as a symbol of national strength and religious zeal. His story, therefore, became integrated into the broader narrative of European Christendom's struggle against Islam, transforming him into a symbolic figure in the larger historical conflict. This framing served nationalistic agendas, often glossing over the complexities of the medieval world and presenting a simplified version of the past that reinforced ideologies. The focus shifted from the realities of his political challenges to his symbolic role as a defender of Christendom against the "infidel." This transition further romanticized his image, often portraying him as an almost mythical figure, a heroic knight-king valiantly defending the Holy Land.

The 19th and 20th centuries saw a resurgence of interest in the Crusades, fueled by romanticism and a new wave of historical scholarship. Historians began to engage more critically with the sources, challenging the simplistic narratives of previous eras. This renewed interest, however, didn't always result in a more accurate portrayal of Baldwin IV. The romanticism of the era often reinforced the already established heroic image, while modern biases toward a more secular interpretation sometimes disregarded the religious and spiritual dimensions of his life and reign. Popular culture, particularly fiction, contributed significantly to this romanticized image, with Baldwin often portrayed as a valiant, if tragic, hero, battling both his illness and his enemies with unwavering courage. These fictional accounts, though not necessarily historically accurate, exerted a considerable influence on the public perception of Baldwin IV, solidifying his image as a legendary figure in the collective memory. This influence extended into the realm of art, where depictions of Baldwin IV often emphasized his regal bearing and military prowess, ignoring or downplaying the physical realities of his leprosy.

The development of modern historical methodology brought a renewed focus on textual criticism and source analysis. Historians started to pay closer attention to the nuances of the original chronicles and to the biases embedded within those narratives. This led to a more nuanced understanding of Baldwin IV's reign, acknowledging both his triumphs and his limitations. His illness, once largely relegated to the background, became a significant factor in the historical analysis of his reign, shaping our understanding of his political strategies and his relationships with his advisors and his court. Yet even this more critical approach hasn't entirely erased the romanticized image built over centuries.

The sheer force of historical memory and popular imagination remains a powerful factor, making it challenging to fully separate the "real" Baldwin IV from the legendary figure who has captivated the public imagination.

The enduring appeal of Baldwin IV's story is arguably linked to the inherent drama of his life. The juxtaposition of his extraordinary achievements with his debilitating illness creates a compelling narrative, resonating with audiences across centuries. His unwavering courage, his military brilliance, and his struggle against overwhelming odds have made him a captivating figure for both historians and the public. This is further complicated by the relative scarcity of surviving visual representations that accurately depict his physical appearance. Most visual representations either minimize or romanticize his physical condition, contributing to the ongoing debate about his actual appearance.

It's also worth acknowledging that the perception of Baldwin IV has been influenced by the cyclical nature of historical interpretations. The Crusades themselves have been interpreted in vastly different ways over time, from periods of uncritical celebration to periods of intense moral scrutiny. These shifts in perception of the Crusades inevitably affect the understanding of key figures like Baldwin IV. When the Crusades were viewed as a glorious period of religious expansion, Baldwin IV was celebrated as a heroic champion of Christendom. When the Crusades were reinterpreted as a complex and often brutal historical phenomenon, the complexities of
Baldwin IV's reign and the moral implications of his actions were more closely examined.

In conclusion, the evolution of Baldwin IV's image from contemporary accounts to modern interpretations showcases the dynamic interplay between historical fact, cultural biases, and popular imagination. While modern scholarships aim for a more

nuanced and accurate portrayal, the legendary aspects of his life continue to shape our understanding. The legacy of Baldwin IV, therefore, remains a compelling testament to the enduring power of history and the fascinating ways in which a historical figure can be reinterpreted and reimagined across centuries. He remains a fascinating subject of study precisely because the "real" Baldwin IV is ultimately inseparable from the layers of legend and myth that have accumulated around his name. The challenge for historians is not to erase these layers but to engage with them critically,
exploring how these various representations have shaped our understanding of this remarkable figure and its impact on the historical narrative of the Kingdom of Jerusalem and the broader context of the Crusades. The ongoing fascination with his life underscores the fact that history is not simply a record of past events but a constantly evolving narrative, influenced by the
context and perspective of each succeeding generation.

Chapter 23

Baldwin IV in Modern Scholarship Recent Interpretations and Debates

The past few decades have witnessed a surge of scholarly interest in Baldwin IV, moving beyond the romanticized portrayals prevalent in earlier historical accounts. This renewed focus has yielded a more nuanced understanding of his reign, challenged simplistic narratives and incorporated recent advances in medieval studies.

Scholars are increasingly examining the interplay between Baldwin's personal struggles with leprosy and his political strategies, challenging the traditional view of him solely as a heroic warrior-king. The debilitating nature of his disease, previously often minimized or ignored, is now recognized as a central factor shaping his decisions, relationships, and ultimately, his legacy.

One area of significant debate revolves around Baldwin IV's character. While older interpretations often portrayed him as an almost saintly figure, unwavering in his faith and exceptional in his leadership, more recent scholarship presents a more complex and multifaceted portrait. Historians analyzed his actions not merely through a lens of heroic virtue but also by considering the political realities of his time and the constraints imposed by his illness. His sometimes-ruthless actions, such as the imprisonment of rivals or his shifting alliances, are now interpreted not simply as flaws but as strategic moves within a complex and highly competitive political landscape. His relationships with his family, particularly his sister Sibylla and his nephew Baldwin V, are scrutinized in greater detail, illuminating the inherent tensions and power struggles within his court. The question of his own ambition and his motivations in shaping succession is also subject to renewed scrutiny, moving beyond the simplified narratives that previously presented his actions as solely dictated by piety or a concern for the welfare of the Kingdom.

The impact of leprosy on Baldwin IV's reign is another area of intense scholarly focus. While earlier works often glossed over the physical realities of his disease, recent scholarship explores its profound influence on his military strategies, his diplomatic maneuvers, and his relationships with his advisors. The progressive nature of his illness, causing increasing physical limitations, necessitated adaptations in his leadership style and approach to warfare. His reliance on trusted advisors, such as Raymond of Tripoli, is increasingly seen not merely as a sign of weakness or indecision but rather as a strategic adaptation to his physical constraints. Historians are also exploring the social implications of his illness, examining how leprosy affected his interactions with his court, his interactions with the populace, and the overall perception of his authority. The impact of his physical appearance and the associated stigma of leprosy on his ability to exercise power is a crucial element in understanding his reign. Recent studies have increasingly acknowledged the societal prejudices against people with leprosy during the 12th century and how these prejudices might have influenced the political dynamics of his court.

The relationship between Baldwin IV and the various factions within his kingdom—the barons, the clergy, and the various competing families—is also a subject of ongoing debate. Some historians emphasize the constant tension between the king and the powerful nobility, highlighting instances of rebellion and opposition. Others focus on Baldwin's skillful management of these conflicts, emphasizing his ability to maintain a degree of order and stability despite the ongoing challenges. The role of religion in shaping both the king's decisions and the perception of his reign is also a central theme in recent studies. The question of how much Baldwin's piety influenced his actions, and how much his actions were interpreted through a religious lens by his contemporaries, is critically examined. Historians are exploring how religious ideology shaped both his political maneuvering and the narratives that emerged after his death. The analysis of primary sources, utilizing advanced linguistic and textual analysis techniques, allows for a more nuanced interpretation of the contemporary accounts, moving beyond simplistic interpretations and uncovering previously overlooked details.

Moreover, recent scholarship examined Baldwin IV's military successes and failures within the broader context of the Crusades. The victory at Montgisard, often presented as a miraculous triumph, is now analyzed with greater attention to the strategic factors and military contingencies that contributed to its success. Baldwin IV's military decisions are examined not just in isolation, but within the context of broader military strategy and the political realities of the kingdom. His losses, like those incurred in the defense of Kerak, are also investigated to understand the limitations of his strategy and the challenges he faced in maintaining the Kingdom of Jerusalem against the expanding Ayyubid forces. This more critical approach moves beyond the triumphalist narratives of earlier accounts and provides a more balanced and realistic appraisal of his military achievements and shortcomings.

The question of Baldwin IV's legacy continues to be debated among historians. Some argue that his short but impactful reign laid the foundations for a period of relative stability in the Kingdom of Jerusalem, despite the inherent challenges and internal conflicts.

Others emphasize the instability that followed his death, arguing that his efforts to secure a stable succession ultimately failed.

Historians are grappling with the extent to which his leprosy shaped his legacy, the impact of his character on the kingdom's subsequent history, and the lasting image projected onto him by subsequent generations. The analysis of visual representations of Baldwin IV, as well as the evolution of his image in literary and artistic portrayals across centuries, contributes to a deeper understanding of his legacy and its subsequent transformation.

The study of Baldwin IV's reign also provides valuable insights into the broader historical context of the Crusader States. His reign is considered not merely in isolation but within the larger context of political, religious, and military conflicts within the Levant during the late twelfth century. His relationships with neighboring Muslim states, his involvement in the wider political dynamics of the region, and the impact of his actions on the balance of power in the Eastern Mediterranean are explored in greater depth. This broader context adds crucial layers to the understanding of Baldwin IV's actions, choices, and legacy. His reign is increasingly seen as an intricate tapestry of personal struggles, political maneuvering, and external threats, all interwoven against the backdrop of a period of significant transformation in the Crusader States.

In conclusion, the modern scholarship on Baldwin IV of Jerusalem demonstrates a marked departure from earlier, largely romanticized interpretations. Recent research offers a multifaceted portrayal of the king, acknowledging the complexities of his character, his reign, and the historical context in which he operated. By employing rigorous textual analysis, considering the impact of his illness, and analyzing his actions within the broader context of the Crusader States, scholars are building a richer and more nuanced understanding of this fascinating and enigmatic historical figure.

While the enduring legend of Baldwin IV persists, the modern historical endeavor continues to strive for a more accurate and comprehensive understanding of the historical reality, acknowledging the biases of earlier interpretations and acknowledging the challenges in disentangling legend from historical reality. This ongoing scholarly engagement with the life and times of Baldwin IV ensures that his story continues to fascinate and inspire, serving as a powerful testament to the dynamic and ever-evolving nature of historical interpretation. The ongoing debates and reinterpretations within the field underscore the significance of continuous critical engagement with historical sources and the complexities of interpreting the past.

Chapter 24

The Impact of his Reign on the Crusader States A LongTerm Perspective

The assessment of Baldwin IV's long-term impact on the Crusader States requires a nuanced understanding, moving beyond simple narratives of triumph or tragedy. While his reign was relatively short, lasting only a decade and a half, its consequences reverberated through the subsequent history of the Kingdom of Jerusalem and the broader context of the Levant. His successes and failures, intricately interwoven, shaped the political landscape, military strategies, and even the cultural perceptions of the Crusader kingdoms for decades to come.

One of Baldwin IV's most significant legacies was his strategic military prowess, demonstrated most vividly at the Battle of Montgisard in 1177. This resounding victory against Saladin's vastly superior army, despite his own debilitating illness, established him as a military genius and a formidable opponent. However, the victory was not simply a matter of luck or divine intervention, as often romanticized in earlier accounts. Modern scholarship emphasizes the meticulous planning, skillful deployment of troops, and shrewd exploitation of terrain that contributed to the Crusader triumph. The impact extended beyond the immediate battlefield; Montgisard bolstered Crusader morale, deterred further immediate Ayyubid advances, and reinforced Baldwin's authority within the kingdom, both amongst the nobility and the populace. His strategic acumen, evidenced by his decisions concerning the fortification of key sites like Kerak, also played a critical role in the protracted defense against Saladin's forces, even in the face of mounting pressure and increasing internal conflicts. This strategic foresight contributed to a prolonged period of relative stability that outlived him, despite the increasing challenges faced by the Crusader states.

Yet, Baldwin IV's military achievements should not obscure the limitations he faced and the ultimate cost. His victories were achieved

against a backdrop of growing Ayyubid power. The defense of Kerak, though ultimately successful during his reign, highlighted the strain on the Kingdom's resources and the growing difficulty of sustaining military campaigns against a formidable enemy like Saladin. His strategies, while effective in the short term, failed to fully address the underlying structural weaknesses of the Crusader states: internal divisions among the nobility, strained relations with the Byzantine Empire, and the growing economic and military might of Saladin's unified Ayyubid empire. His death, therefore, left the kingdom vulnerable to the Ayyubid advances that ultimately culminated in the Fall of Jerusalem in 1187. The
prolonged struggle for control of resources and territories, evident even during his reign, proved a more significant long-term challenge than any single military campaign.

Beyond the military sphere, Baldwin IV's reign profoundly shaped the political dynamics of the Kingdom of Jerusalem. His deft
handling of powerful noble factions, including the ambitious Raymond III of Tripoli and his own family members, demonstrates his political acumen. His reliance on Raymond, often interpreted as a weakness, may be more accurately viewed as a pragmatic alliance necessary for navigating the complex web of power within his court. Baldwin recognized and managed the inherent tensions among the barons effectively, preventing outright rebellion during the most crucial periods of his reign. However, this skilled
management did not eliminate underlying conflicts, only delaying the eventual eruption of internal strife after his death. The
succession crisis that followed, marked by the struggles between Sibylla, Guy de Lusignan, and the regency council, serves as a stark reminder of the fragility of the political order that he had painstakingly maintained. The inability to resolve the dispute in a manner that ensured a peaceful transition of power arguably represents a significant failure in his long-term strategic planning.

The impact of his leprosy on his political maneuvering should not be underestimated. While it undoubtedly presented physical limitations, it also arguably fostered certain aspects of his leadership style. His reliance on trusted advisors, his meticulous planning, and his need to carefully manage his public appearances necessitated strategies that arguably enhanced his political effectiveness in specific circumstances. The perception of his illness, however, inevitably shaped the political landscape, creating opportunities for rivals and sowing the seeds of instability. The very fact that his physical limitations led to such constant negotiation and political manipulation underscored the precariousness of his authority, a problem that amplified after his death, leading to the disastrous consequences of the reign of his successors.

The legacy of Baldwin IV also extends to the realm of religious and cultural influence. His piety and devotion to Christianity were undeniable, yet they coexisted alongside his pragmatic political decisions. The image of him as a saintly king, battling against overwhelming odds, was constructed and reinforced by chroniclers writing in the immediate aftermath of his death. Later religious interpretations of his reign and his persona continued to promote this image, but modern scholarship is reevaluating this traditional narrative, examining the religious context of his rule with a greater sensitivity to political factors. His actions were simultaneously framed by religious beliefs and by the pragmatics of a king struggling to maintain a fragile kingdom in a constantly shifting political environment. Religious interpretations, therefore, cannot be separated from the broader political and military circumstances that shaped his reign and its outcomes.

Finally, the long-term assessment of Baldwin IV's reign necessitates considering its place within the broader history of the Crusader States. His efforts to maintain a semblance of order and stability in the face of rising Ayyubid power served as a crucial, if temporary, bulwark against the increasing instability in the Levant. While his military victories and political maneuvering bought the Kingdom of Jerusalem crucial time, they could not ultimately prevent the eventual setbacks that followed his death. His reign highlights the intricate interplay between internal conflicts and external threats that characterized the late twelfth-century Crusader experience. The challenges he faced, both internal and external, reflect not only the specific circumstances of his time, but also the intrinsic difficulties faced by the Crusader kingdoms throughout their existence.

In conclusion, Baldwin IV's reign, despite its brevity, left a complex and lasting impact on the Crusader States. His military successes bought time, but did not solve the inherent structural weaknesses of the kingdom. His political acumen fostered relative stability, but did not prevent the succession crisis. His pious devotion resonated in the religious narratives surrounding his reign, but it did not override the pragmatism of his political decisions. While he is rightly celebrated as a brilliant military strategist and a skillful politician, the long-term assessment of his impact reveals both triumphs and limitations that continue to shape historical interpretations and fuel debate among scholars. The study of his reign remains vital for understanding not only the specific challenges faced by the Kingdom of Jerusalem in the twelfth century, but also the broader complexities of the Crusader experience and its lasting significance in shaping the history of the region. His story is not a simple tale of heroic triumph or tragic failure, but a complex narrative of skill, struggle, and the limitations of even the most exceptional rulers in a period of extraordinary challenges.

Chapter 25

The Enduring Appeal of Baldwin IV A Symbol of Resilience and Leadership

The enduring fascination with Baldwin IV, King of Jerusalem, extends far beyond the confines of academic historical circles. His story resonates with audiences across centuries and cultures, captivating readers and viewers with its blend of tragedy, triumph, and unwavering determination. This persistent interest stems from several interconnected factors, all contributing to his status as a compelling and enduring symbol.

Firstly, Baldwin IV embodies the archetype of the heroic underdog. Facing a debilitating and stigmatized illness from a young age, he not only overcame significant physical limitations but also rose to become a powerful and effective ruler. His triumph over adversity, both physical and political, offers a powerful message of resilience and perseverance, appealing to audiences who appreciate stories of overcoming the seemingly insurmountable. The stark contrast between his physical frailty and his impressive military and political accomplishments serve as a potent narrative device, emphasizing the strength of his will and the limitations of societal prejudice against those with disabilities. This narrative, particularly relevant in modern discussions of disability and empowerment, continues to resonate with contemporary audiences, fostering a renewed appreciation of his accomplishments beyond the purely medieval context.

Secondly, his reign offers a compelling study in leadership during a period of intense conflict and crisis. Facing the formidable threat of Saladin's rapidly expanding Ayyubid empire, Baldwin IV displayed remarkable strategic acumen and military prowess. The Battle of Montgisard, a stunning victory against overwhelming odds, remains a cornerstone of his legacy, illustrating his capacity for bold decision-making and inspired battlefield leadership. His ability to inspire loyalty and cooperation among his often-fractious barons, despite the inherent challenges of his illness and the internal political intrigues within his kingdom, underlines his exceptional political skills. His careful cultivation of alliances, his pragmatic approach to diplomacy, and his understanding of the political dynamics of the Crusader States, all contributed to a relatively stable period within the kingdom despite the looming Ayyubid threat. The careful balancing act he performed between religious piety and shrewd political pragmatism, between his own health and the demands of his responsibilities, showcases an exceptional ruler navigating an exceptionally difficult situation. These qualities, often lacking in contemporary leaders, render Baldwin IV's story particularly relevant and inspiring, providing a powerful case study in effective leadership under immense pressure.

Moreover, the tragic element inherent in Baldwin IV's life significantly enhances his appeal. His premature death, exacerbated by his illness, left his kingdom vulnerable to the very forces he had fought so tirelessly to contain. The poignant contrast between his exceptional achievements and the ultimately devastating consequences of his demise serve as a powerful reminder of the fragility of power and the limitations of even the most talented rulers. The succession crisis that followed his death, further highlighting the instability he had managed to suppress during his reign, only amplifies the tragic dimension of his story. The ensuing chaos ultimately led to the devastating loss of Jerusalem, a stark reminder of his efforts, which, though temporally successful, could not completely counter the larger historical forces at play. His life and death provide a compelling narrative of human resilience in the face of both internal and external threats, a narrative that transcends mere historical analysis and strikes a chord with a broader audience through its emotionally resonant themes.

Further contributing to his enduring appeal is the wealth of primary source material pertaining to his life and reign. Chroniclers such as William of Tyre provide detailed accounts of his reign, painting a vivid picture of his personality, his achievements, and his struggles. These contemporary accounts, while often influenced by the biases of their authors, nevertheless provide valuable insights into the political, military, and social contexts of his life. Modern scholars have meticulously analyzed these sources, building a more nuanced and complex understanding of Baldwin IV beyond the often romanticized or simplified portrayals that emerged in the centuries following his death. This rich historical record allows for a deeper and more informed engagement with his story, allowing us to better appreciate the complexity of his character and the challenges he faced. The ongoing scholarly debate surrounding his reign and legacy further enhances his importance as a case study, generating ongoing interest and ensuring his continued relevance to historical scholarship.

Finally, the enduring appeal of Baldwin IV lies in his symbolic significance as a figure representing both triumph over adversity and the limitations of human power. His story transcends its medieval context, offering a timeless message of resilience, leadership, and the inevitable intersection between personal struggle and historical forces. He serves as a powerful reminder that even the most remarkable individuals are ultimately subject to the constraints of their circumstances, while simultaneously inspiring audiences with the potential for human greatness in the face of seemingly insurmountable obstacles. His legacy, therefore, extends beyond the realm of medieval history, becoming a source of inspiration and reflection for audiences across time and cultures, ensuring that his story continues to captivate and resonate for generations to come. The ongoing interest in Baldwin IV underscores not only his historical significance but also the enduring power of narrative and the human desire to find inspiration in tales of courage, resilience, and the ultimately tragic, yet undeniably compelling, aspects of the human condition. His enduring legacy is not solely one of military strategy or political maneuvering, but one that embodies the human spirit's remarkable capacity for perseverance in the face of insurmountable odds. This lasting appeal firmly establishes Baldwin IV as a figure whose story continues to resonate with profound and enduring significance.

Chapter 26

Primary Sources Chronicles Letters and Contemporary Accounts

The meticulous reconstruction of Baldwin IV's life and reign hinges critically on the careful analysis of primary source material. These sources, while imperfect and often biased, provide invaluable glimpses into the political, social, and military realities of the twelfth-century Kingdom of Jerusalem. They offer a multifaceted portrait of the king himself, his relationships with his contemporaries, and the challenges faced by his kingdom. However, understanding their limitations is as crucial as understanding their content. The inherent subjectivity of historical sources necessitates a critical approach, one that weighs the author's perspective, their potential motivations, and the context in which the accounts were created.

Among the most significant primary sources are the chronicles of the period. William of Tyre's *Historia rerum in partibus transmarinis gestarum* stands out as a particularly important text. Written by a participant in the events he describes, William, Archbishop of Tyre, provides a detailed and relatively contemporary account of Baldwin IV's reign. His work offers valuable insights into the political machinations, military campaigns, and internal conflicts that characterized the kingdom during this period. However, it is important to acknowledge William's position as a participant in these events and his clear biases. His account is often favorable towards the Latin-speaking population and the ruling elite, potentially overlooking or downplaying the experiences and perspectives of other groups within the kingdom. His proximity to power inevitably shaped his narrative, influencing both his choice of information to include and his presentation of the events he witnessed.

Another crucial chronicle is that of Ernoul, a continuation of William of Tyre's work. Ernoul offers a different perspective, frequently critical of certain actions and policies of the royal court. His perspective, though less comprehensive than William's, provides a counterpoint and allows historians to consider alternative interpretations of events. The comparative analysis of William of Tyre and Ernoul's accounts ~~reveals~~reveal inconsistencies and ~~allows~~allow for a richer, more nuanced understanding of the historical record. Their differing viewpoints highlight the importance of consulting multiple sources to create a balanced historical narrative. Neither chronicle provides a completely unbiased account, but their combined use offers a more comprehensive understanding than either could provide alone. Their contrasting perspectives, coupled with the scrutiny of modern historical scholarship, enable us to approach the past with caution and greater precision.

Beyond chronicles, letters and other contemporary documents illuminate aspects of Baldwin IV's life and reign that are not always found in the more formal narratives. Papal correspondence, for example, provides insights into the political and religious dynamics of the Crusader States and their relationship with the papacy. These letters often reveal the urgent concerns of the time, the anxieties about the growing power of Saladin, and the pleas for military assistance from Europe. They provide a sense of urgency and immediacy, often absent from the more deliberate chronicles.

Furthermore, analyzing the language and tone of these letters reveals the complex web of political alliances and rivalries that characterized the period. The subtle nuances of diplomacy and the veiled criticisms found within these documents offer a glimpse into the behind-the-scenes power struggles of the Crusader kingdom.

The surviving letters written by or to Baldwin IV himself are unfortunately few. The scarcity of these primary documents further underscores the challenge of reconstructing a complete picture of the king's inner thoughts and motivations. However, even a small collection of his correspondence could still offer crucial insights.

These letters would provide a firsthand perspective on the king's decision-making processes, his diplomatic interactions with various leaders, and his personal views on critical political issues. The absence of a substantial corpus of the king's correspondence does not diminish the significance of those documents that have survived, making them even more precious and deserving of careful scholarly analysis.

In addition to chronicles and letters, contemporary accounts from other sources provide valuable supplemental information. These

may include accounts from participants in military campaigns, reports from envoys, and even travelogues from pilgrims. While not always as detailed or comprehensive as the chronicles, these
documents often provide vivid snapshots of life in the Crusader States, offering details about daily life, social structures, and the experiences of individuals within the kingdom. These accounts, often fragmented and sporadic, contribute to a broader understanding of the context in which Baldwin IV reigned, supplementing the more formal narrative accounts provided by the chronicles. The collective picture assembled from these various accounts is far richer and more comprehensive than any single source could offer. The task of the historian is to synthesize these diverse perspectives, weighing their strengths and limitations to arrive at a nuanced understanding.

The evaluation of primary sources demands a nuanced and critical approach. Historians must consider the author's background, their motivations, and potential biases. William of Tyre, for instance, was a clergyman and an active participant in the political life of the kingdom. His account reflects his own position and his commitment to the Latin Crusader community. Similarly, Ernoul's account, though less formal, reveals his own opinions and assessments of the events he narrates. By acknowledging these biases, historians can create a more objective interpretation, comparing sources to identify areas of agreement and disagreement.

Furthermore, the physical condition of the surviving sources must be considered. The manuscript tradition often involves copying and recopying texts, introducing potential errors and variations over time. Scholars must carefully analyze different manuscript versions to identify any discrepancies and evaluate their significance. They often use paleographic techniques to date the manuscripts and identify scribal practices. Determining the authenticity and dating of the source material is a crucial initial step before undertaking any substantive analysis of the historical accounts. This process requires specialized knowledge and skills, highlighting the
importance of interdisciplinary collaboration in historical research.

Finally, understanding the limitations of the sources is paramount. The surviving primary sources provide an incomplete picture of

Baldwin IV's reign. Many documents have been lost or destroyed over time, and the perspectives of many individuals and groups remain unrepresented in the surviving accounts. The surviving accounts are overwhelmingly from the perspective of the Latin-speaking elite, reflecting a cultural and social bias. This inherent limitation requires historians to acknowledge the gaps in the historical record and to interpret the available evidence cautiously.

The challenge lies in piecing together a coherent narrative from often fragmentary and sometimes contradictory sources. The historian's task is not simply to present the facts as found in the sources but also to critically analyze and interpret them,
acknowledging their biases and limitations, and drawing informed inferences from the available data. This process of careful evaluation and synthesis is at the very heart of historical scholarship and is crucial to the construction of a responsible and reliable biography of Baldwin IV.

Chapter 27

Archaeological Evidence Material Culture and its Insights

Archaeological evidence offers a crucial, albeit often silent, counterpoint to the written historical record. While chronicles and letters provide invaluable insights into the political and social dynamics of the Kingdom of Jerusalem during Baldwin IV's reign, archaeological findings offer a tangible connection to the material culture of the period, enriching our understanding of daily life, military technology, and the broader societal context in which the king operated. The scarcity of specifically Balduinian sites dedicated solely to him, however, necessitates a broader approach to archaeological evidence, focusing on the material culture of the Kingdom during his reign (1174-1185).

The fortifications of the Crusader states, for instance, provide a wealth of information. Archaeological excavations at numerous castles and cities across the Levant, such as Krak des Chevaliers, Château Pèlerin, and the city walls of Jerusalem itself, reveal not only sophisticated military architecture but also insights into construction techniques, logistical capabilities, and the economic resources available to the kingdom. The scale and complexity of these fortifications, many of which were strengthened or expanded during Baldwin IV's reign, reflect the kingdom's ongoing struggle for survival against the encroaching forces of Saladin. Analysis of the materials used in construction – the type of stone, the mortar, the timber – can reveal trade networks, access to resources, and even seasonal variations in construction activity. Detailed studies of siege weaponry unearthed during excavations, such as the remains of catapults and mangonels, provide insights into military technology and its evolution during this period of intense conflict.

Beyond fortifications, the domestic architecture of the Crusader states also offers valuable clues. Excavations of residential buildings in cities like Acre and Tyre provide evidence of daily life, revealing information about living conditions, social structures, and economic activity. The size and layout of buildings, the materials used in their construction, and the types of artifacts found within them offer insights into the social stratification of Crusader society. For instance, the discovery of luxurious imported goods in certain residents suggest a wealthy elite, while the more modest dwellings reflect the living conditions of the common people. The discovery of workshops and craft production sites helps us understand the local economy and its relationship to both local and international trade networks.

Ceramic finds are particularly revealing. Pottery shards, a ubiquitous element in archaeological contexts, offer valuable chronological information and insights into trade patterns. The presence of locally produced pottery alongside imported wares provides insights into economic exchange and cultural interaction. Analysis of the style, form, and decoration of pottery can be used to establish chronological sequences and to identify distinct cultural influences. The identification of specific types of pottery that are associated with time periods and regions helps contextualize other finds and build a more accurate picture of the social and economic landscape of the kingdom. The sheer volume of ceramic material unearthed in numerous sites across the Kingdom provides a rich source of information that, when systematically analyzed, significantly enhances our comprehension of the economic and social structures of the period.

The study of metalwork also holds immense significance. The remnants of weapons, tools, and personal adornments unearthed during excavations provide evidence of metallurgical practices and technological advancements during the period. The analysis of the alloys used in these objects, as well as their style and decoration, reveals trade patterns and cultural interactions. The discovery of high-quality metalwork, such as intricately crafted jewelry or weaponry, often indicates wealth and craftsmanship. Such finds can inform us about the artisanal skills that flourished in the Crusader kingdoms, revealing the sophistication of the kingdom's metalworking industries.

Similarly, the analysis of grave goods provides insights into burial practices, social hierarchies, and religious beliefs. Excavations of cemeteries have revealed the diverse range of individuals who lived in the Crusader states, from common soldiers to high-ranking officials and clerics. The objects buried with the deceased – weapons, jewelry, clothing fragments – reflect their social status, their religious beliefs, and their personal possessions. The study of grave goods provides a more nuanced understanding of the diverse population that made up the kingdom, going beyond the often-elite-focused accounts in written sources. This nuanced understanding helps flesh out the complexities of society and provides a richer and more complete picture of daily life during Baldwin IV's reign.

However, the interpretation of archaeological evidence requires caution. The context of discovery is of paramount importance. The location of an artifact, its association with other objects, and the stratigraphy of the site all contribute to its interpretation.

Furthermore, the limited excavation of many sites and the destruction of many others through urban development or modern conflict hinder the reconstruction of a comprehensive picture. It is crucial to acknowledge the limitations of the available data and avoid generalizing based on incomplete evidence.

Furthermore, the relationship between written and archaeological evidence is often complex and sometimes contradictory.

Archaeological findings can support or challenge the narratives presented in chronicles and letters. In cases of contradiction, the historian must weigh the evidence carefully, considering the strengths and limitations of both types of sources. The combination of written and archaeological evidence offers a more holistic and nuanced approach to understanding the past. This interdisciplinary approach, combining textual analysis with archaeological investigation, allows for a more robust and multifaceted understanding of the Kingdom of Jerusalem during Baldwin IV's reign, enriching our historical narrative.

The study of numismatics, or coins, also offers a unique perspective. The coins circulated during Baldwin IV's reign provide insights into the kingdom's economy and its monetary policies. The images and inscriptions on these coins often reflect the king's authority and the political climate of the time. The analysis of coin circulation patterns can help map trade routes and understand the economic reach of the kingdom. The metallurgical analysis of the coins provides insights into the materials and techniques employed in their manufacture, reflecting the economic resources and technological capabilities of the mint. This provides a unique

insight into the practical realities of administration during the reign of Baldwin IV. By examining these various dimensions of material culture – from fortifications to coins – we can better grasp the material realities of the Crusader Kingdom and how those realities shaped Baldwin IV's reign, offering a richer and more complete narrative than solely relying on written sources. The silent voices of the archaeological record, when carefully listened to, complement and occasionally challenge the eloquent pronouncements of written history, creating a more robust and nuanced understanding of Baldwin IV and his tumultuous era. The combination of these approaches allows historians to approach a richer and more
compelling narrative, one that is not limited by the biases or perspectives of the authors of the written record but is informed and enhanced by the material remains of the kingdom itself.

Chapter 28

Secondary Scholarship Major Works and Interpretations

The study of King Baldwin IV and the Crusader states benefits immensely from a rich secondary scholarship, offering diverse interpretations and perspectives on his reign and the broader historical context. This section surveys major scholarly works, categorizing them thematically to highlight key contributions and ongoing debates. Understanding these diverse interpretations is crucial for a nuanced appreciation of Baldwin IV's legacy.

One significant area of scholarly focus centers on Baldwin IV's reign itself. Steven Runciman's, *A History of the Crusades,* while not solely dedicated to Baldwin IV, provides a foundational narrative, setting the king's reign within the larger context of the Crusader states' struggles against Muslim powers. Runciman's work, though influential, has been subject to critique for its Eurocentric biases and occasional reliance on limited sources. More recent scholarships have attempted to address these shortcomings, incorporating a wider range of sources and perspectives. For instance, Christopher Tyerman's *God's War: A New History of the Crusades* offers a more comprehensive and nuanced assessment of the crusader ideology and its impact on the political and social dynamics of the Crusader kingdoms, providing crucial background for understanding the complexities of Baldwin IV's rule. Tyerman's detailed analysis of the religious and political motivations of the crusaders offers a sophisticated understanding of the challenges Baldwin IV faced.

Further explorations into Baldwin IV's life and reign frequently focus on his remarkable resilience in the face of leprosy. Several works, while not always explicitly biographical, indirectly illuminate this aspect. For example, studies on the social and medical aspects of leprosy in the medieval period offer insight into the challenges Baldwin faced and how his illness may have shaped his political strategies and personal relationships. These studies often draw on medical texts, chronicles, and even archaeological findings of leper colonies to provide a broader context for understanding Baldwin IV's experience. The impact of leprosy on his leadership is debated; some scholars argue it strengthened his resolve and strategic thinking, forcing him to rely on advisors and fostering a unique style of leadership that involved delegating authority effectively while retaining ultimate control. Conversely, others point to the constraints it placed upon his activities and suggest that it accelerated his decline and the eventual unraveling of his kingdom.

The political landscape of the Crusader states during Baldwin IV's reign forms another significant area of scholarly investigation. The intricate web of alliances, rivalries, and power struggles among the various factions within the kingdom are extensively documented. Bernard Hamilton's work, particularly his contributions to the Oxford Dictionary of National Biography, provides detailed biographies of key figures in Baldwin IV's court, offering insights into the personal relationships and political maneuvering that characterized his reign. Understanding these relationships and rivalries is crucial to interpreting Baldwin's political actions and strategies. Scholarly works often examine the crucial role played by Raynald de Châtillon, and his impact on the precarious balance of power with Saladin, ultimately contributing to the kingdom's later instability. The tensions between the different baronial families, particularly the differences between the ambitions of Raymond III of Tripoli and those of other lords, frequently feature in these analyses, highlighting the complexities of governing the kingdom during such a tumultuous time.

Beyond the internal politics of the Kingdom, the external threats posed by Saladin and the Ayyubid dynasty dominate many scholarly works. The military strategies employed by both Baldwin IV and Saladin are analyzed meticulously, often focusing on specific battles such as Montgisard. These analyses frequently explore the tactical brilliance of Baldwin IV, particularly his use of terrain and cavalry in his famous victory against a larger Ayyubid army. Such studies highlight not just his military prowess, but also his diplomatic skill and understanding of military strategy despite his health. In contrast, others explore the growing strength of Saladin's forces, demonstrating the persistent threat to the Crusader kingdom's existence. The interplay between these military campaigns and political negotiations forms a crucial aspect of understanding the dynamics of this conflict. Recent scholarship has emphasized the importance of understanding both sides of the conflict, moving away from earlier narratives that presented the Crusades primarily from a European perspective.

The succession crisis following Baldwin IV's death is another frequently studied topic. The struggles between Sibylla, Baldwin V, and Guy de Lusignan have been examined in detail, revealing the internal divisions and political machinations that ultimately contributed to the kingdom's downfall. Scholars delve into the motivations of these key players, examining their personal ambitions and the role of the various noble houses in shaping the course of the succession crisis. This period has received significant attention, as it demonstrated the fragility of the kingdom and its vulnerability to internal conflict at a critical juncture. The analysis of the events leading to the fall of Jerusalem in 1187 frequently includes discussions of the role of the succession dispute in weakening the kingdom and contributing to its eventual defeat by Saladin.

Moreover, the broader context of the Crusader states, their economic structure, and their relationship with the surrounding Muslim societies, are essential elements addressed by the secondary scholarship. Works on the economic organization of the Crusader kingdoms, including trade, agriculture, and urban development, provide insights into the kingdom's infrastructure and its ability to withstand external threats. Understanding this economic landscape is crucial for appreciating the challenges faced by Baldwin IV and the resources available to him. Studies on the cultural exchange between the Crusader kingdoms and the neighboring Muslim states reveal the complex interactions and mutual influences that shaped the identity and character of the Crusader states. This cultural interaction went beyond mere conflict, incorporating intellectual exchange and the adoption of various aspects of the local culture by both sides.

In conclusion, the secondary scholarship surrounding Baldwin IV, the Crusader states, and the broader context of the twelfth century Levant offers a rich and multifaceted understanding of this pivotal historical period. While older works often present a Eurocentric perspective, more recent scholarship strives for a more balanced and nuanced approach, drawing on a wider range of sources and

incorporating the diverse perspectives of the different societies involved. This continuous evolution of interpretation, fueled by new discoveries and methodological advancements, ensures that the study of Baldwin IV's reign and the fate of the Crusader kingdoms remains a dynamic and engaging area of historical inquiry,
constantly revealing new insights and challenging established narratives. The careful consideration of these diverse scholarly works is essential for gaining a thorough and comprehensive understanding of this remarkable king and his turbulent era. The interweaving of political, military, social, economic, and religious factors within this scholarship provides a holistic appreciation for the challenges and triumphs of Baldwin IV and his kingdom. This multi-faceted approach ensures a more complete picture of the period than a solely biographical approach could provide. Future research will continue to refine our understanding of this critical period in history, building upon the considerable achievements of previous scholars.

Chapter 29

Historiographical Debates Key Controversies and Unresolved Questions

The study of Baldwin IV and the Crusader States is not without its scholarly controversies. While a substantial body of work offers a rich tapestry of information, several key areas remain subject to ongoing debate and interpretation. Understanding these historiographical disputes is crucial for navigating the complexities of this fascinating period and appreciating the nuances of Baldwin IV's legacy.

One significant area of contention revolves around the precise extent of Baldwin IV's influence on political and military decisions. While his strategic brilliance at Montgisard is widely acknowledged, the degree to which his illness affected his ability to govern remains a subject of debate. Some scholars argue that his leprosy, while debilitating, fostered a pragmatic and effective leadership style characterized by astute delegation of authority and reliance on trusted advisors. They emphasize his ability to maintain control despite physical limitations, highlighting his political acumen and his understanding of the limitations imposed by his condition.

Examples such as his calculated use of his illness to garner sympathy and support, or his careful manipulation of power struggles among his barons, are often cited as evidence of his continued effectiveness.

Conversely, other historians contend that his illness progressively impaired his decision-making capabilities, ultimately contributing to the kingdom's instability. They point to the escalating power struggles within the court and the kingdom's increasingly precarious position during his later years as evidence of this decline in effectiveness. These scholars highlight the influence of powerful barons like Raynald de Châtillon and the growing divisions within the nobility as factors that weakened the kingdom's position, arguing that Baldwin IV, weakened by his illness, was increasingly unable to effectively counter these challenges. They propose that his inability to decisively resolve the succession crisis laid the groundwork for the catastrophic events that followed his death. The balance of influence between the disease and the king's strategic maneuvering is therefore an important and ongoing debate in the field.

Another point of scholarly contention centers on the nature of Baldwin IV's relationship with his advisors and the extent to which they influenced his decisions. The roles of figures like Raymond III of Tripoli and William of Tyre, for example, have been subjected to varying interpretations. While some portray them as loyal and supportive advisors who acted in the best interests of the kingdom, others suggest their motivations were more self-serving, highlighting the potential for manipulation and the complexities of courtly politics. The extent to which these advisors truly reflected Baldwin IV's own desires or exerted their own agendas remains a subject of ongoing debate. The challenge lies in discerning the king's true intentions from the biased accounts provided by contemporary chroniclers, often deeply involved in the political machines themselves. This creates a challenge for modern historians seeking to establish an objective interpretation of events.

The interaction between the Crusader states and the surrounding Muslim societies also generates considerable historiographical debate. Early interpretations often presented a stark dichotomy between Christian crusaders and Muslim adversaries, perpetuating a narrative of religious conflict and conquest. However, more recent scholarship has challenged this simplistic view, emphasizing the complexities of intercultural interactions. These more nuanced perspectives highlight the significant economic and cultural exchange between the two societies. Trade, diplomatic relations, and cultural influences shaped the landscape of the Crusader states in profound ways, challenging the notion of a purely antagonistic relationship. Historians are increasingly exploring these areas, utilizing diverse sources including Arabic chronicles, archaeological evidence, and economic records, to provide a more comprehensive understanding of these relationships. The complexities of this interaction call into question the simplistic narratives which once dominated this field.

The depiction of Saladin in historical narratives is another controversial area. While earlier accounts often portrayed him as a monolithic figure of ruthless ambition, more recent scholarship offers a more nuanced perspective, acknowledging his military prowess and strategic acumen alongside his political and religious motivations. The analysis of his campaigns, including his interactions with the Crusader states, often focuses on his strategic brilliance, his diplomacy, and his attempts to unite the various Muslim factions under his rule. His religious piety and political pragmatism, often portrayed separately, are increasingly discussed as intertwined motivations driving his actions. These interpretations move beyond simple demonization to a more complex understanding of his role in the conflict and his place in history.

The fall of Jerusalem in 1187 and its preceding events are frequently analyzed through different lenses. While older interpretations attributed the kingdom's downfall primarily to military defeat, newer analyses suggest that internal divisions, political instability, and the ongoing succession crisis played a far greater role in weakening the Crusader kingdom and paving the way for Saladin's victory. The balance of external military pressure and internal political weakness in leading to the fall of Jerusalem is a point of continuing academic disagreement. The debate revolves around the relative weight of these factors in understanding the collapse of the Crusader kingdom. Some argue that Saladin's military victories were inevitable given the kingdom's inherent weaknesses, while others suggest that with better internal cohesion, a different outcome may have been possible.

The sources themselves are a crucial element of these debates. The reliance on primarily Latin chronicles, which often present a Eurocentric perspective, has been a subject of ongoing criticism.

The incorporation of Arabic sources, however, has offered alternative perspectives and enriched the historical narrative.

Reconciling these different viewpoints and interpreting contradictory accounts remain a significant challenge for historians, requiring a critical evaluation of bias, perspective, and the limitations of the available historical record.

In conclusion, while the life and reign of Baldwin IV and the history of the Crusader states have been extensively studied, numerous unresolved questions and controversies continue to fuel scholarly debate. The understanding of the interplay between his illness and his leadership, the true nature of his relationships with his advisors, the complexities of intercultural interactions, the multifaceted nature of Saladin, and the causes of the kingdom's eventual fall all remain areas of ongoing discussion and interpretation. The exploration of these controversies underscores the dynamic and evolving nature of historical scholarship, highlighting the importance of critical analysis, diverse perspectives, and a continuous reevaluation of existing interpretations. The study of this period continues to evolve as new sources are discovered and new methodologies are applied to existing data. This ensures the continuing vitality of the scholarly study of the Crusader kingdoms and the life of this remarkable medieval king.

Chapter 30

Further Research and Resources Continuing the Exploration

This book explores the life and reign of Baldwin IV, King of Jerusalem, a figure whose life was as dramatic as the era in which he lived. His story, interwoven with the complexities of the Crusader States, offers a fascinating lens through which to examine the political, military, and social dynamics of twelfth-century Palestine. However, the narrative presented here represents only a starting point for a deeper understanding of this pivotal period. To further enrich your knowledge and continue this exploration, I encourage you to engage with the rich array of primary and secondary sources that are available.

For the dedicated academic, delving into primary sources offers an unparalleled opportunity to engage directly with the historical record. While many sources are available in translated versions, accessing the original Latin, Arabic, and Armenian texts provides a deeper appreciation of the nuances and subtleties often lost in translation. The works of William of Tyre, a contemporary chronicler whose *Historia rerum in partibus transmarinis gestarum* provides a detailed account of the events of Baldwin IV's reign, represent a crucial starting point. His perspective, while undeniably shaped by his position within the Crusader court, offers invaluable insights into the political machines and military campaigns of the time. However, it's crucial to approach William of Tyre, as with all primary sources, with a critical eye, recognizing potential biases and limitations in his narrative. His account needs to be corroborated and contrasted with other contemporary sources to get a more complete picture.

Equally important are the Arabic chronicles, which offer a contrasting perspective on events. These sources, often written from the perspective of Muslim observers and participants, provide crucial insights into Saladin's strategies, motivations, and perspectives on the conflict. These contrasting accounts allow for a more nuanced understanding of the interactions between the Crusader States and their Muslim neighbors, moving beyond simplistic narratives of religious conflict. Accessing and analyzing these Arabic texts requires linguistic expertise, but translations are increasingly available, making them accessible to a wider audience.

The works of Ibn al-Athir and Baha al-Din ibn Shaddad are particularly valuable in this regard, providing detailed accounts of Saladin's campaigns and his relationship with the Crusader kingdoms. Careful comparison of the Latin and Arabic accounts allows for a richer, more complex, and balanced understanding of this tumultuous period.

Beyond chronicles, the exploration of other primary sources can significantly deepen understanding. Papal documents, for instance, provide insights into the relationship between the Crusader States and the papacy, revealing the political and religious dynamics influencing events in the Holy Land. Seals, charters, and other archival materials offer glimpses into the day-to-day functioning of the Crusader States, revealing details of administration, economic activity, and social structures. These sources, often preserved in archives across Europe and the Middle East, provide invaluable evidence for understanding the intricate workings of society during this period. Accessing these materials often requires travel to archives and specialized knowledge, but many institutions are increasingly digitizing their collections, making them more accessible online.

For those seeking a less intensive engagement with the historical record, a wide array of secondary sources offers excellent introductions and detailed analyses of Baldwin IV's life and the Crusader States. Numerous biographies of Baldwin IV offer differing interpretations of his reign, highlighting his accomplishments and struggles. These works often draw on both primary and secondary sources, providing a more accessible entry point into the complexities of his life and the historical context in which he operated. Similarly, numerous scholarly studies on the Crusader States offer detailed analyses of the political, military, social, and religious aspects of this fascinating period. These works often delve into the intricacies of the interactions between the Crusader kingdoms and their neighbors, exploring the cultural exchanges, economic relationships, and conflicts that shaped the region.

Beyond books and academic journals, numerous online resources can further enhance one's understanding. Websites of major

~~archives~~Archives and libraries often provide access to digitized primary sources, allowing researchers to examine original documents without needing to travel to the physical locations. Online databases such as JSTOR and Project MUSE offer access to scholarly articles and books, providing a wealth of information on various aspects of Crusader history. Furthermore, numerous websites and online communities are dedicated to medieval history, providing forums for discussion, sharing resources, and engaging with others interested in this period. These online communities represent a dynamic space for expanding one's understanding and engaging in scholarly discourse.

Several key areas warrant further investigation. The nature of Baldwin IV's illness and its impact on his leadership continues to be debated. While his leprosy undoubtedly presented significant physical challenges, the extent to which it affected his political and military decisions remains a topic of ongoing discussion. Exploring this topic requires careful consideration of both contemporary descriptions of his condition and interpretations of his actions in the context of his illness. Similarly, the relationships between Baldwin IV and key figures within his court – such as Raymond III of Tripoli and William of Tyre – require further scrutiny. Understanding the dynamics of power within the Crusader court requires an analysis of their motivations, actions, and influence on Baldwin IV's decisions.

The relationship between the Crusader States and their Muslim neighbours is another richly complex area deserving of further study. While the conflicts are well documented, the significant economic and cultural exchanges that occurred need more exploration. Further investigation requires utilizing a wider range of sources, including Arabic chronicles and archaeological evidence, to construct a more balanced picture. Furthermore, the nature of Saladin's leadership and his strategic approach to the conflict require a more detailed analysis. His motivations, both religious and political, are explored in numerous sources, but a comprehensive understanding requires synthesizing multiple perspectives and interpretations.

In addition to these specific topics, readers can explore broader themes related to the Crusader States. These could include analyses of the legal systems, economic structures, social dynamics, and religious practices that characterized these fascinating societies. The study of architecture, art, and literature of the period is particularly important to appreciate the material culture of the Crusader States. By exploring these wider themes, you'll acquire a fuller understanding of the period.

Finally, it is crucial to remember that historical understanding is not static. As new evidence emerges and interpretations evolve, our understanding of Baldwin IV and the Crusader States will continue to develop. Critical engagement with different viewpoints, a rigorous approach to source analysis, and a commitment to intellectual honesty are essential for a deeper appreciation of this fascinating period. The resources mentioned above offer a starting point for this ongoing exploration. By continuing to engage with primary and secondary sources, critical discussions, and ongoing scholarly research, you can contribute to the ever evolving understanding of this pivotal moment in history. The journey into the past, and the exploration of Baldwin IV's life, is a continuous one. I hope this chapter has sparked your curiosity and motivated you to engage in this ongoing scholarly quest.

Acknowledgments

This book would not have been possible without the generous support and guidance of numerous individuals. My deepest gratitude goes to Professor Eleanor Jane Siddons of the University of Oxford, whose insightful comments and unwavering encouragement throughout the research and writing process were invaluable. I am also indebted to Dr. David Jacoby of the Hebrew University of Jerusalem, whose expertise on the Crusader states proved essential in shaping the narrative. The staff of the British Library and the National Archives of France provided exceptional assistance in accessing and navigating crucial primary source materials. Finally, my sincere thanks to my family and friends for their patience and understanding during the long years of research and writing.

Appendix

Appendix A: Genealogical Chart of the House of Anjou and its connections to the Kingdom of Jerusalem.

Appendix B: Map of the Crusader States in the 12th Century, showing key locations and battle sites mentioned in the text.

Appendix C: Transcription of a selected passage from William of Tyre's *Historia rerum in partibus transmarinis gestarum* relating to Baldwin IV's reign, including a brief analysis of its historical context and potential biases.

Glossary

This glossary provides definitions for key terms used throughout the book relating to medieval society, military organization, and the political landscape of the Crusader States:

Bayt al-Maqdis: Arabic name for Jerusalem.

Emir: A title used for a Muslim military commander or regional ruler.

fief: A landed estate granted to a vassal in exchange for military service.

Leper: A person afflicted with leprosy, a chronic infectious disease.

Saracen: A medieval term used to refer to Muslims, particularly those in the Middle East.

Sultan: A title used for a Muslim sovereign or ruler, often with supreme authority.

vassal: A person who pledged loyalty and military service to a lord in exchange for land or other benefits.

References

This section lists all the works cited in this biography. The full bibliography is available online at [Insert Web Address Here]. A shortened list of essential reading is included below:

William of Tyre, A History of Deeds Done Beyond the Sea.
Ibn al-Athir, The Chronicle.
Baha al-Din ibn Shaddad, The Life of Saladin.
Steven Runciman, A History of the Crusades.
Christopher Tyerman, God's War: A New History of the Crusades.
Joshua Prawer, The World of the Crusades.

Author Biography

Sir Jerry Brewer received his Knighthood from the Knights Templar of Great Britain as the Minister of the United States and published a Book and numerous articles the Knights Templar.

Printed in Great Britain
by Amazon